RASHMI LUTHRA

GROWING UP IN RURAL INDIA
Problems and Needs of Adolescent Girls

GROWING UP IN RURAL INDIA

Problems and Needs of Adolescent Girls

RANJANA KUMARI
RENUKA SINGH
ANJU DUBEY

Advent Books, Inc., New York

Financial support for this study was provided by USAID, New Delhi.

First Published 1990

ISBN 0-89891-035-8

Library of Congress Catalog Card No. 88-82785

Printed in India.

Contents

List of Tables

Acknowledgements

The present study owes its fruition from the origin to its completion to the efforts and support of Dr. (Mrs.) Sharada Jain, Honarary Secretary, Sevagram Vikas Sansthan, Bharatpur, Rajasthan. I thank her profusely.

Mrs. C.P. Sujaya, Joint Secretary, Department of Women and Child Development, Ministry of Human Resources Development, Government of India, and Dr. Saramma Mathai of USAID can grin in satisfaction for whatever rigour and merit there is, in the study; I shall bear the remorse for its demerits. They have been highly forthcoming throughout the study to advise us on the implied nuances and problem - shifts at every stage of planning of the study and analysis at every stage of the study which otherwise may have gone unnoticed. I wish to congratulate them both, and thank USAID and the Department of Women and Child Development, for the funding support.

Dr. Ravi Chopra (CSR), Dr. T.N. Jha (NABARD), Dr. Divakaran (CSR), Dr. (Ms.) Manjula Rathaur (CSR), Dr. Anand Kumar (BHU), Dr. Indrani Ganguly (VHAI) Dr.S. Gopalan (Nutrition Foundation of India), Dr. W.B. Rogers Beasley (USAID), Dr. Urmil Goel (NIPA), Dr. Leela Dubey of Nehru Memorial Museum and Library and Dr. Sarojini Bisaria (NCERT) whose critical, intellectual and methodological inputs helped the study a long way, are remembered here with gratitude.

Dr. Renuka Singh, Anju Dubey and N. Varadarajan formed the core of the research team and the researchers and invesigators (named separately elsewhere) their exension into the remotely placed villages and their people. I owe them my sincere gratitude.

This study has been a valuable experience to me. I am grateful to all those including my family, who made it all possible.

I thank Balakrishnan for his patience in rushing through the typing, repeatedly and often from an illegible maze of manuscripts.

RANJANA KUMARI

Chapter One

Introduction

With simultaneous pressures from both national and international fora, the hitherto most neglected section of Indian society, women, have of late started receiving the attention of the policy makers and planners in India. It was for the first time in the Sixth Five Year Plan that 'development of women' was recognised as a national task. This emphasis continues in the Seventh Five Year Plan. As a result, several programmes have been initiated to benefit women. While this is a welcome step forward the development initiatives taken so far to benefit women can by no means be called adequate. In particular, girls between the stage of childhood and adulthood who are often called 'adolescents' continues to be grossly neglected. Even after decades of planning and socio-economic development programmes, they continue to languish without recognition, status and educational, employment and social opportunities and rights, let alone the opportunity for participation in decision making and self development.

Indian society is still reluctant if not vehemently opposed to give due importance to these young girls despite the fact that it is they who will eventually not only become mothers, but have many familial, economic and social responsibilities. In short, they will be playing a significant role in shaping the character of future generations.

Denied of any control over their own bodies, adolescent girls are often led to unwittingly become mere instruments of reproduction. Denied of education and awareness, they are condemned to lead a culturally, nutritionally, emotionally and economically sterile life. The early deprivations of all kinds that they are subjected to cannot but lead them to emerge as already socially crippled adults. In fact, most maladies, debilities and problems, of adult women can be traced back to their adolescence period. This is the reason for paying special attention to the proper intellectual, biological and social development of adolescent girls. The saying that 'a stitch in time saves nine' is nowhere more relevant and true.

Adolescent girls form a considerable proportion of India's future human resources. It is thus vital to ensure their proper development. This, of course, cannot be done unless we understand the forces of the factors that shape or affect their personality development. The adolescent period is one which is marked by intense biological, psychological and physical changes and turbulence. It is also the most critical period for learning, and receptivity to awareness. This stage is also marked by changes in intellectual abilities of problem perceptions and problem solving. But at the same time, it is also a stage which needs various inputs of right content and quality. We need to know also the forces which place limitations on their awareness levels. An intensive study of these issues and problems in real life situations will go a long way in helping the planners with the critical decision-making inputs for the development of this section of our national population.

The Universe of Adolescence

The years of adolescence are the years of change - of development at the biological, psychological and social level. This is a period when girls start menstruating, get married and some of them have their first child, especially in the rural areas. In other words, these are the years of maturation, of acquiring new social roles and responsibilities. It is in these years of passage from childhood to womanhood that a girl perhaps needs maximum attention to enable her to be healthy and productive in later life. Yet this age group has been neglected so far. Although much is being said and done about the development of women, the girl child who will grow into a woman remains a much neglected entity.

Etymologically speaking, the term "adolescence" originates from the Latin word *adolescere* which means 'maturing' or 'to grow up'. The growth could be physiological, psychological and/or social. From a biological point of view, "adolescence is the period extending from puberty to the attainment of full reproductive maturity. Different parts of the reproductive system reach their maximal efficiency at different stages in the life-cycle; and strictly speaking, adolescence is not completed until all the structures and processes necessary to fertilization, conception, gestation and lactation have become mature."[1]

Psychologically, adolescence refers to a period of identity-crisis. Crisis, however, does not mean a breakdown or catastrophe but rather a "crucial" period when development must move one way or another and when stable reference points in and around the young persons must be established. Generally the identity concept focuses on the integration of a number of important elements - such as capacities, opportunities, ideals and identifications into a viable self-definition.[2]

According to Hollingshead, adolescence is the period in the life of a person when the society in which he/she functions ceases to regard him/her as a child, while not according him/her a full adult status, roles and functions. Adolescence, in the sociological sense is related to the experience of passing through the unstructured and ill-defined phase that lies between childhood and adulthood. In terms of behaviour, adolescence is defined by the social roles a young person is expected to play, is allowed to play, is forced to play or prohibited from playing because of his or her status in society. Sociologically, the important thing about the adolescent years is the way the maturing individual is regarded and influenced by the society. The physiological changes such as the development of the breasts and other secondary manifestation of adolescence in the female and the less obvious changes in the male connected with sex-maturation such as rapid growth, voice changes, the appearance of labial, axial and pubic hair derive their significance from the way they are regarded by the society in which the adolescent lives.

The adolescent has a peculiar 'midway' status; he or she is no longer a child but he or she has not acquired adult social, legal or economic status either. As a quasi-child yet, simultaneously, a quasi-adult, he or she is faced with many dilemmas.[3]

It has been observed that even a legal declaration of adulthood does not necessarily mark the end of adolescence. According to Sebald, the major elements that signal the termination of adolescence are:

a) sociologically, the termination of status discontinuity
b) psychologically, completing a number of developmental tasks and achieving a modicum of consistent identity
c) biologically, achieving physiological maturity
d) legally, reaching the age limit specified by law
e) economically, becoming self-supporting and maintaining a balance between production and consumption
f) traditionally, when informal customs lift the last restriction on adult privileges.[4]

The literature on urban adolescents in India reveals 16 years and above as the age of sharp discontinuity in life. Compared to the urban adolescent girl, the marriage of a rural young girl takes place early, specially once she has reached puberty.

Adolescence in Indian Rural Society

There seems to be a consensus amongst psychologists, anthropologists and sociologists regarding the socio-cultural circumstances affecting the onset of adolescence. Adolescence can be curbed or possibly altogether avoided when the society provides or imposes an alternative role. In a society where there is a sense of belonging to a cultural tradition, the meaning of adolescence will differ, and change only gradually.

Sebald's study on adolescence indicates that the various socio-economic systems offer different roles to the young. In an agrarian society one may not find typical adolescence but would find youth. In the industrial society, on the other hand, one would find adolescents who are at cross-roads to select their roles. In the post-industrial society, there would be adolescents, youth sub-culture and even a counter-culture.[5]

The first generalisation seems to be true of the Indian rural situation where we do not find typical adolescent girls but just young girls. There is no space for adolescence to occur in such rural situation as has been understood in the western model or even the Indian-urban reality. The studies on urban adolescents concentrate on feelings of deprivation and denial; feelings of exclusion and exile; feeling of remorse, shame and guilt; of control and helplessness in its face; feelings of sacrifice of the parents which demands complete surrender and gratitude, yet tinged with a sense of rebellion; feelings of awkwardness intermixed with dependence and rejection; feelings of loneliness when there is nobody to turn to in moments of distress as characteristics of urban adolescents. This is a result of the shift in family roles and sharp break in life space along with the experience of alienation.[6]

However, in the rural context, we find that the girl takes up the adult role immediately around or after reaching puberty. In the rural families, the stabilizing source is the economic role of the parents. The emotional communication amongst the family members in rural areas hardly leaves any scope for experiencing a crisis peculiar to the urban adolescents.

Young Girls in Rural India -- Objective Reality

The young girls who are the subject of this study, are the most ignored section of Indian society. The discrimination against them begins right from birth. Today, with amniocentesis tests being used not merely to detect deformities in the foetus but gender as well, and many parents demanding abortion of female foetuses, we may say that discrimination starts before birth itself.

The child in India is viewed as a divine gift. The birth of a child is not merely an expression of the biological unity between the parents but cements the psychological unity of the family. The first child brings joy to the family. However, if it happens to be a girl, mixed feelings are expressed even though in the ancient Hindu tradition the first child, if it is a girl, is supposed to bring luck to the family. Much attention has been given to the girl or *kanya* by Manu, and in the Indian epics.

The most natural and fairest calling for a girl is said to be that of a loving wife and a tender mother. But, however important woman is, her entry into the city of life is seldom hailed with hosannas and palmstrewn roads, nor is she met with the blare of trumpets that joyfully greets the warrior-hero. She is neither a world redeemer nor a world shaker, but *Samsarahetu*, the "source of the world".[7]

Some families do welcome the birth of the girl child but the majority lays particular emphasis on the first child being a boy. The husband experiences an affirmation of his masculinity in the birth of a son. More so, because in the Hindu religion, man's salvation comes only through his son. The daughter, however, is seen to bring happiness only through her sons and that is always an uncertain thing.

Most of the parents treat their daughters as economic liabilities because when they get married they will take away with them part of the family resources as dowry. Girls are also unwanted as they represent potential sexually active beings that could prove to be threatening to the mothers. The sons, on the other hand, are treated as assets and superior to girls because of the economic benefits they would provide to the family once they are gainfully employed. In our patriarchal and patrilineal societies they are also seen as vital for ensuring the continuity of the family line.

Such attitudes are the genesis of discrimination against girls even before birth. The practice of femicide, i.e. killing of the girl foetus, is all too common, specially amongst the well-to-do classes in the urban areas.

This is supported by statistical evidence on gender based differences in infant mortality rates in India. Female infants are considered biologically superior to males in their ability to survive. However, in our country "this seems to be true of only the first week or the first month of life after which the female-death-rate takes over."[8]

According to a UNICEF report,[9] the child mortality rates for little girls (1-4 years and 5-14 years) are higher than that for little boys, in almost all states except Andhra Pradesh and Tamil Nadu, where the two rates are almost equal.

Interestingly, the percentages of deaths in rural areas for all ages and for most of the listed causes such as child-birth and pregnancy (maternal deaths), fevers, digestive disorders, disorders of respiratory system, disorders of central nervous system and circulatory system and causes peculiar to infancy are considerably higher for females than for males. The all-India figures for deaths by all causes for 1983 shows a ratio of death rates between males and females of 16.5 and 17.2 for below one year children, 6.5 and 9.4 for 1-4 years, 4.2 and 5.0 for 5-14 years, 3.8 and 5.6 for 15-24 years, and 4.5 and 6.1 for 25-34 years.[10] A classification of major states in India according to pre-natal mortality (infant deaths within seven days per 1000 live births) between 1976-78, shows that Kerala has the lowest figure (below 20) in rural areas, while Andhra Pradesh showed a death rate of more than sixty. This is more so in the peak reproductive age of mothers of 15-29 years. It has been attributed to the hazards of pregnancy, among several other possible causal factors.

Table 1.1: Age Sex Distribution of Reported Deaths: Number and Percentage (all India, 1980)

Age Group	Persons	Males	Females
5-14 years	963 (5.4)	474 (4.9)	489 (6.1)
15-24 years	800 (4.5)	349 (3.6)	451 (5.6)
Total (all ages, 0-70 years)	16,848 (100.0)	8,991 (100.0)	4,857 (100.0)

Source: Office of the Registrar General, *Survey of Causes of Death (Rural)*, 1980.

Various studies[11] indicate a mortality rate for the girl, (6.1 for 5-14 years age group and 5.6 for 15-24 years age group) which is more than that of boys (4.9 and 3.6 per cent for the same age groups). This difference in the morality rate reflects the importance given to the male child. The higher female mortality rate is perhaps due to the negligence and discrimination on the part of the family in providing adequate nutrition and preventive and curative health care. Despite the evidence of higher morbidity among female children, attendance records at OPDs and clinics reveal a preponderance of male children. This could be because of the immediate attention and medical care given to the male children, unlike the females who get delayed medical care and that also only in case of an emergency. Most of them are left to the mercy of nature. Not only does the principle of scarcity determine the neglect of the girls in the lowest rung of rural society but the imitation of the socio-cultural traditions of the upper castes trends to circumscribe the lives of the lower caste people that results in the percolation of sexism at various levels.

Discrimination also exists in regard to the nutrition of the girl where parents do not give attention and proper care. They fail to realise that she has to be healthy herself in order to be a healthy mother and worker. This discrimination is also partly due to the parents' worry about having to get her married off once she starts menstruating. A delayed menstruation postpones the urgency or concern of the parents.

Discrimination in Education

Education is another area where parents are usually inclined to spend less on the daughters than on their sons. One reason for this could be because the son's education is directly linked with his prospect of employment. Secondly, parents expect sons to look after them in their old age. Thirdly, it is only the sons who will continue the family lineage according to religious understanding.

Today there is an increasing change in the attitudes of the parents with regard to the education of the girl. However, look at the female literacy rates for the country as a whole, and adolescent girls in particular, shows continuing wide differences in the educational development of boys and girls. The enrolment figures by age and class (Table 1.2, 1.3), drop-out rates and secondary school achievement and retention rates (Graph I) lend support to this.

Table 1.2: Percentage of Children in the Age-Group 6-11, 12-14, 15-17 enrolled in schools

Year	Primary Education		Middle Education		Secondary Education	
	Boys	Girls	Boys	Girls	Boys	Girls
1971	76.69	48.96	36.97	17.69	22.92	09.56
1981	79.84	54.32	42.88	24.32	28.62	14.06

From Table 1.2 it is clear that, whereas, there has been an increase in the enrolment of girls at the primary, middle and secondary levels from 1971 to 1981, this increase is not significant when compared to the respective figures for the boys. For instance, for the year 1981, 54.32 per cent girls were enrolled at the primary level against 79.83 per cent of the boys. For the middle and secondary levels, these figures are 24.32 per cent as against 42.88 per cent for boys and 14.06 per cent as against 28.62 per cent respectively.

Moreover, there is a sharp fall in the percentage of girls enrolled at the secondary levels. Whereas it is 54.32 per cent at the primary level, it falls to 24.32 per cent at the middle and 14.06 per cent at the secondary level. This is in conformity with the trends shown with regard to the retention rates at different stages in different states (Table 1.3 and Graph I)

A comparison of the enrolment level achieved in different states indicates the enormity of the task to be accomplished by the relatively backward states. In Rajasthan, for instance, 70 per cent of the girls in the age group 6 to 11 years are not at school and of the age group 11 to 14 years, 89 per cent of the girls have not been enrolled. While enrolment figures for all scheduled caste and scheduled tribe children are generally low, the figures for girls tend to be much lower than that for boys in these communities.

Table 1.3: School Enrolment by Educational level and Sex (all India: 1981-82)

Class	Enrolment figures and percentages		
	Boys	Girls	Total
Age Group 6-14 (elementary stage, classes I-VII)	58,947,833 (83.59%)	35,670,915 (53.55%)	94,618,748 (68.99%)
Age Group 14-17	8,044,300 (33.47%)	3,510,086 (15.61%)	11,545,386 (24.85%)

Drop Out Rates

According to the 1975 Report on educational development by the Committee on the Status of Women in India:

- in classes I to V, one girl out of three was attending school and of every 100 girls enrolled only 30 reach class V

- in classes V to VII only one girl out of five was at school

- in the age group 14 to 17 years, only 12 per cent were enrolled

- the drop out rate for girls was 62 per cent at the lower primary stage as against 56 per cent for boys. At higher primary stage, it was 34 per cent as against 24 per cent for boys. 'Wastage and stagnation' were 62.3 per cent for boys and 71.4 per cent for girls in primary and middle schools.

The drop out and repeat rates are much higher for girls (74 per cent) than for boys (62.4 per cent). The majority of the girls drop out at the primary level. Within the primary level, this rate is highest at grades I and II as the following Table indicates.

Table 1.4: Drop out rates for girls

Primary Grades	Percentage
I - II	42.35
II - III	12.02
III - IV	8.51
IV - V	7.88

The figures with regard to secondary school achievement of girls between ages 14 and 17 are:

Table 1.5: Secondary School Achievement of Girls between ages 14 and 17 in '000

Boys in class 12	6,648.5 (66.9%)
Girls in class 12	2,842.6 (23.1%)
	9,499.1

At the secondary level, sustained enrolment of girls is 13 per cent, against 35 per cent for boys. The proportion of girls enrolled at this stage has now dropped to 1 in 8. Secondary education for girls is, for the most part, confined to the upper middle classes in urban areas. Girls in rural areas constitute only 17 per cent of total enrolment in secondary classes.[12]

Although the ratio of female to male literacy was 44 per cent in rural areas, for the different age cohorts, by the level of education, the differentials are very high. For example, for the 5-9 age cohort, the ratio was 35.1 and 25.8, for 10-14 years, 66.9 and 44.8, for 15-19, it was 66.1 and 43.3, for the 20-24 it was 66.5 and 37.2. This reflects, that at higher levels of literacy, starting from secondary schools, the percentage of literates among women is considerably low, as compared with that of boys.[13]

Our study also confirms higher drop out rate of girls in the rural areas, especially during the adolescent period. Sharp discontinuities in their roles occur at this juncture. This sort of educational experience combined with the socialisation process of the young girls in rural areas leads to the perpetuation of low self-esteem.

Pushed into Early Marriage

Early marriage is another trend prevalent in the rural areas. The urgency to get the girl (who is usually perceived as a temporary resident of her natal home) married off, is not merely because she is treated as a burden but also because of the belief, particularly amongst the upper castes, that once the girl starts menstruating she becomes capable of reproducing. Therefore, if she is not married off, the father is held guilty of killing the seeds which could have been fertilized.

Moreover, the parents do not wish to risk endangering the reputation of the girl and consequently of the family. This customs of marrying off of girls, as soon as possible, after puberty, though common to all castes, is most strictly observed by the Brahmins as well as as Rajputs. Once a girl has passed the marriageable age it is very difficult to find a husband for her.

However age is not a significant factor in increase of dowry in most communities. Often, the dowry demands may reflect the level of vulnerability of the girl's parents with aged unmarried daughters and the taboos, responsibilities and sense of guilt associated with them.

Soon after puberty, there are restrictions imposed on the young girls in terms of mobility and consumption of certain types of 'hot' food (supposed to stimulate sexual appetites). Notions of purity and pollution are introduced strictly in connection with menstruation.

Despite the fact that the legal age at marriage for the girls is 18 years, many girls are being married off much before that, specially in the rural areas. This generally leads to early pregnancy for which the young girl is physiologically and psychologically unprepared. Socio-culturally the girl is indoctrinated and passes from childhood to womanhood. During this process, however, physically and mentally she is unprepared to perform the role of a wife and a mother. Early marriage in rural areas results from a strong sense of insecurity springing from the fear of abuse and sexual harassment. Thus, marriage is seen to be the most appropriate response in such circumstances.

Premature Pregnancy and Maternal and Infant Mortality

The decade of the seventies undoubtedly saw the proportion of married girls in the age group 15-19 decrease by nearly a quarter from the level prevailing in the sixties, i.e. 55 per cent. But this has still left 43.47 per cent of the 15-19 years old married in 1981, and more (48.92 per cent) in rural areas. While the national average age at marriage is showing increase, the situation in Rajasthan, Bihar, Madhya Pradesh and Uttar Pradesh is that the proportion of those married in the age group 15-19 has remained as high as 64.25, 64.06, 62.71 and 60.5 per cent respectively, showing a mean age of marriage at 17. The situation in rural areas is still worse. Statewise figures for the proportion of married within the age group of 10-14 year old girls show an average of 6.59 of this tender age group, rural figures showing a greater proportion.[14]

Apart from disastrous demographic consequences, the early marriage of girls has severe implications for their health. Various studies have shown that the capacity for reproduction is not synchronous with menarche and puberty. Full sexual maturity and stability in growth as opposed to the mere development of reproductive capacity is not earlier than 18 years in girls, and among the deprived, undernourished communities not earlier than 19 years. ICMR studies[15] show that while Indian girls attain reproductive capacity between the ages of 16-19, sexual maturity and stability in physical growth adequate for reproduction are attained only about the age of 18 or 19. Dr. Gopalan's study, on the basis of analysis of mean heights and weights of girls of ages 15-19, shows that at age 15, as many as 49-67 per cent would be at risk during pregnancy on account of being below the minimum standards of weight and height, and that child-birth is very hazardous for mothers under 20. Mortality rate was as much as 418 per every 100,000 live births, and according to a WHO study it may range from 200 to 1200 for India as a whole and as much as 592 for Alwar District in Rajasthan.

Further, for each maternal death there were 16.5 illnesses related to pregnancy, childbirth and puerperium for this age group, according to a longitudinal survey in India between 1974-79. And yet almost seven per cent of girls between 10-14 years and 43-46 per cent of girls between 15-19 age group are married. Maternal age has a strong relationship with infant mortality which is high for young mothers under 20, lowest for mothers aged between 20-30 and rising thereafter. A Delhi study has shown that neonatal mortality was more than double among teenage mothers, compared with 20-24 year olds. In fact, most studies confirm a high risk of infant deaths faced by young mothers below 20 years. Studies also show that mothers under 15 faced a perinatal maternal mortality rate of 166.7 per 1000 deliveries, mothers aged between 20-29 years 68.5, and mothers under 15 years about 171 deaths. In India, infant mortality is highest in states where the age of marriage is low - U.P., M.P. and Rajasthan.

Pregnancy before 19-20 is marked by a high incidence of pregnancy wastage through abortion, still birth and neonatal deaths. Even when the infant survives, children born to women under 18 suffer other damaging forms of ill health which can permanently harm a child such as through low birthweight risk of prematurity, difficult deliveries and even chromosomal anomalies, neural tube defects, etc.

Need to Study the Status of Young Girls

It is clear that young girls in rural areas are strongly discriminated against in terms of access to food, nutrition, health and education. A girl, having a secondary status and a low self-image, ignorant and neglected becomes an important subject of study as it would be pertinent to see as to what sort of future-mother and future-worker she would grow to be. What will be her role in shaping up the future village society? Moreover, this study becomes relevant as it would enable us to bridge the data-gap that exists on this section of the population. It is also a timely study keeping in mind, firstly, the fact that experts and planners concerned with the problems of women in development have, hitherto, paid rarely any adequate attention to the problems of rural adolescent girls. Secondly, the objectives and emphasis of the Seventh Plan on the socio-economic programmes for women rarely have identified those relevant to them.

This study on the problems and needs of adolescent girls is a significant contribution to the existing sociological literature on the status of women in India. It will help in identifying areas for interventionist programmes for the adolescent girls in rural areas which is crucial for the following reasons.

* The majority of the adolescent girls are inhabitants of rural areas, and they form a large but neglected section of population (see Tables 1.6 and 1.7)
* Because of the widespread rural poverty, illiteracy, lack of nutritional and health care, educational and other infrastructural facilities for self development and healthy living in the rural areas, this section of adolescent girls are subject to deprivations of all kinds.
* The period of adolescence, taken as 10-16 years in this study, is a transit stage between childhood and adulthood, and it is a period of active personality development, in physical, intellectual and psychological terms.

Table 1.6: Population Projection by age, All India

Age group in years	1981			1986		
	total	male	female	total	male	female
0 - 4	970857	495875	474982	1053753	540502	513233
5 - 9	921455	474304	447151	920960	471889	449071
10 - 14	827690	433036	394654	910966	469118	441848
	(100.00)	(52.4)	(47.6)	(100.0)	(51.5)	(48.5)
15 - 19	694593	362957	331636	820363	429502	390861
	(100.00)	(52.3)	(47.7)	(100.0)	(52.4)	(47.6)
10 - 19	1522283	795993	726290	1731329	398620	832709
	(100.00)	(52.35)	(47.65)	(100.00)	(51.95)	(48.05)

All ages 0 - 70	6851590 (100.00)	3443843 (57.8)	3307747 (48.20)	7610701 (100.00)	3927868 (49.3)	3862833 (50.7)

Source: *Report of the Expert Committee on Population Projections*, Office of the Registrar General of India, 1986.

Sex ratio by age group in India; Source: *Census of India 1981*. Series 1, India, Registrar General of India, 1984

Number of males per 1000 females

Age group	0 - 4	5 - 9	10 - 14	0 - 14	All age groups
No. of males	1044	1061	1097	1066	1071

Table 1.7: Percentage distribution of estimated population by age groups and sex 1983

Age Group	Rural			Urban			Combined		
	Male	Fem-ale	Total	Male	Fem-ale	Total	Male	Fem-ale	Total
0 - 4	13.35	13.54	13.44	11.93	12.47	12.19	13.03	13.30	13.16
4 - 9	13.35	13.25	13.30	12.27	12.44	12.35	12.85	12.33	12.60
10 - 14	13.18	12.46	12.83	11.70	11.84	11.77	12.85	12.33	12.60
15 - 19	10.77	10.08	10.44	10.93	10.99	10.96	10.81	10.28	10.65
Average for all these groups	12.66	12.33	12.50	11.70	11.99	11.81	12.38	12.06	12.23

Source: Ministry of Home Affairs, Office of the Registrar General, Vital Statistics Division. Sample Registration System 1983.

* Denial of the experience of passage through this period of adolescence amounts to denial of opportunities for personality development and growth of their creative faculties, a pre-condition for a successful, confident, socially productive, biologically active, physically mature later adult life. Such denial will have serious adverse consequences on the health, physical-biological and social-psychological maturity as they

enter adulthood.

* The status of adolescent girls in rural areas is one of helplessness and deprivation of growth possibilities. So far this cohort has not received adequate attention from the planners or administrators or development programmes.
* It is relevant to be able to clearly identify and define the causes and forces that leave them to this status of depravity, as also the areas and forms of intervention to help restore their development opportunities.

Composition of Enrolment by Class
At elementary stage (in thousands)

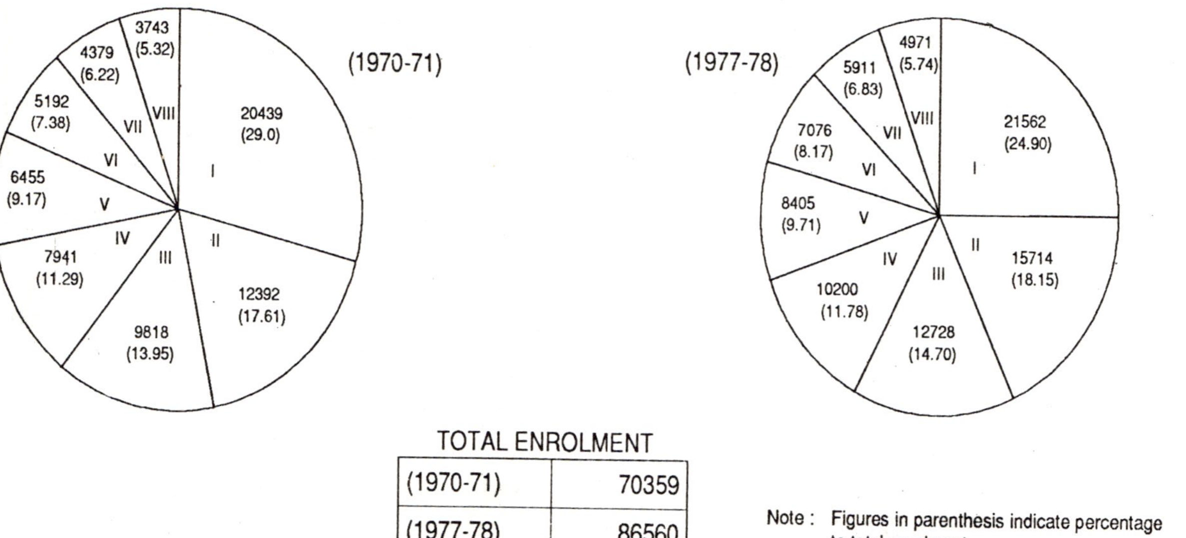

TOTAL ENROLMENT

(1970-71)	70359
(1977-78)	86560

Note : Figures in parenthesis indicate percentage to total enrolment

RETENTION CAPACITY OF PRIMARY SCHOOLS, 1978
Enrolment in Grades II to V as percentage of enrolment in Grade I

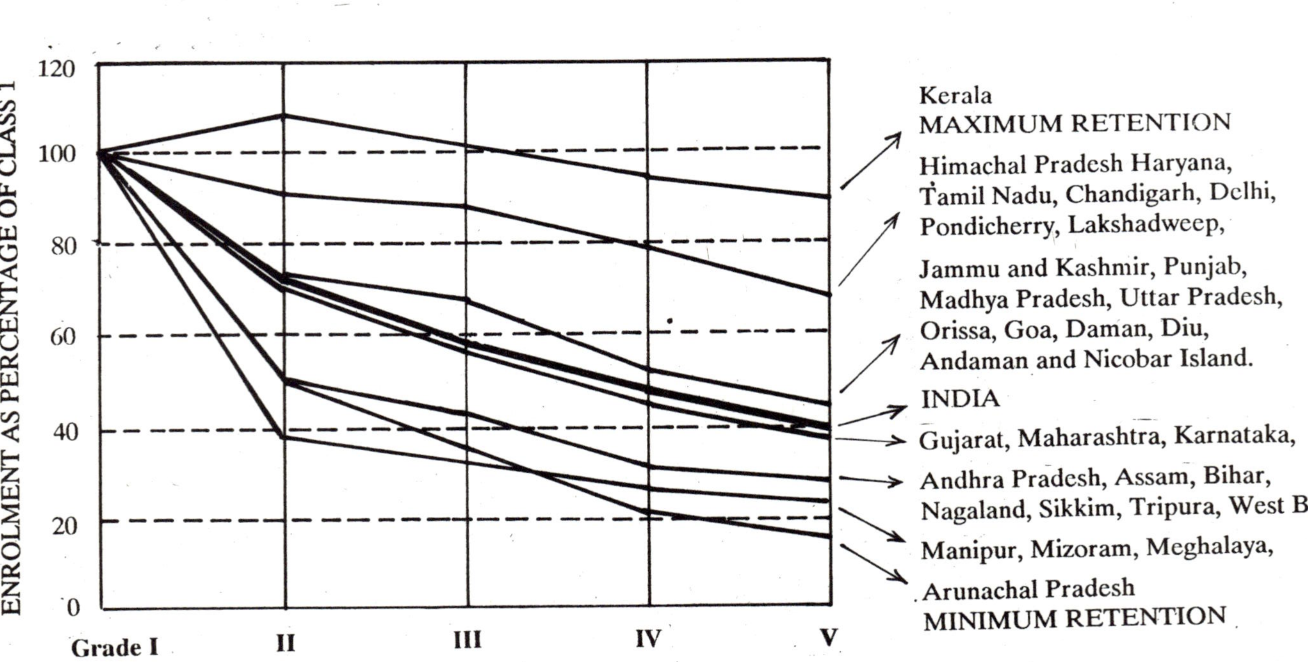

Note: State/Union Territories with

Chapter Two

Research Design

The broad framework of data/information required for the present purpose is related to the socio-demographic characteristics of the subjects, their parents' socio-economic background and perceptions regarding their daughters' education, and general awareness and the village environment. Probing into their problems, hopes and aspirations, their perceptions about health, education, marriage and related issues, is called for. Such information about adolescent girls is rudimentary (where it exists). There is thus an urgent need for an empirical study to collect the required primary data, and an appropriate research design, whose characteristic features are discussed below.

Selection of Villages

The criteria adopted for the selection of the villages to be studied were: (i) the level of infrastructural development/facilities in the village, and (ii) distance from the city. The selected villages were also to form a continuum from the semi-urban (near to the city) to the extremely remote.

Accordingly, the two villages included for study in the sample from the Union Territory of Delhi form the semi-urban type, while the six villages from Bharatpur District in Rajasthan form the less urban villages, and the four villages from Jaunpur District in Uttar Pradesh constitute what may be called the most rural and isolated type. While they may appear to have no territorial contiguity, our preliminary studies, visits, and census records show and confirm that development wise, these three groups of villages or rather the people residing there are at different levels of development, viz. in terms of having access to facilities and economic opportunities.

List of Selected Villages

District/State/Villages	
1. Delhi:	(1) Kishangarh, (2) Rangpuri
2. Bharatpur (Rajasthan):	(1) Malahe, (2) Malipura, (3) Sewar, (4) Noh, (5) Noganya, (6) Peepla
3. Jaunpur (Uttar Pradesh):	(1) Heerapur, (2) Banspha, (3) Baghela, (4) Ramnagar

Unity of Study

The stage of adolescence is generally understood to start around the onset of puberty. In rural India, as several studies have revealed, the average age at puberty is 12 years. However, the social responsibilities and adult roles are assigned to the girl child right from the age of 8-9 years. Also, social and family prescriptions of 'Do's and 'Don'ts' for them start around the same age in a rural setting. The average age at marriage in rural areas coincides more often than not with the year of attainment of puberty. Most girls bear their first child by the age of sixteen. For convenience's sake we have considered the phase of adolescence for a girl to fall somewhere between 10 to 16 years of age, and they form the first unit category for analysis in our study.

We chose the parents as a second category unit, as an analysis of their attitudes and opinion was also thought essential since they not merely influence but even determine the life pattern of these young girls in terms of their educational opportunities (when and upto which level they can study), the age at which they would get married, their mobility within the household and outside, what work would they do and when, etc.

Sample Size

A sample of 400 adolescent girls was considered to be fairly representative. Under the circumstances of many limitations imposed on the study, this number was thought to be the most feasible.

Selection of Sample

In the preliminary stage the adolescent girls were identified with the help of Gram-Pradhan and other elders in these villages. Basic socio-economic information was then sought so as to categorise them in different caste and income groups. From this a further selection was made of thirty-three girls from each village, except Rangpuri in Delhi where 37 adolescent girls were selected. Due consideration was also given to caste, income, marital status, education and family size while selecting the sample. It may be clarified that selecting uniformly 33 girls from each village was done keeping in view the possibility of implementing the programme in future.

Table 2.1: Village-wise size of Sample Selected for the Study

Name of Village	Approx. No. of Households	Available population of adolescent girls	Girls per family	Number and percentage of selected girls
DELHI				
Rangpuri	600	292	0.48	37 (12.7)
Kishangarh	350	158	0.45	33 (20.9)
Total	950	450	0.46	70 (16.8)
RAJASTHAN				
Malahe	312	153	0.49	33 (21.6)
Malipura	208	88	0.42	33 (37.5)
Sewar	486	207	0.42	33 (16.0)
Noh	184	83	0.45	33 (39.8)
Noganya	207	92	0.44	33 (35.9)
Peepla	378	162	0.42	33 (20.4)
Total	1775	605	0.44	198 (8.5)

UTTAR PRADESH				
Heerapur	170	85	0.50	33 (38.8)
Banaspha	139	68	0.48	33 (48.5)
Baghela	171	85	0.49	33 (38.8)
Ramnagar	340	152	0.44	33 (21.7)
TOTAL	820	475	0.47	132 (36.95)
Grand Total	**3445**	**1530**	**0.45**	**400 (27.4)**

Techniques of Data Collection

We felt that in order to present a rounded picture, we should collect both quantitative and qualitative information regarding the problems and needs of adolescent girls in rural areas. The bulk of the quantitative information was generated through a structured questionnaire. This was supplemented by group discussions and on-the-spot observation.

The process of formulating the questionnaire on the 'problems and needs of adolescent girls in rural areas' was a challenging task. It was difficult in terms of identifying visible and invisible needs and associations that would describe her situation in totality, more so because there is little much literature in this area.

The almost intractable problem of getting an adequate response from an age group of girls who were quite shy and not very articulate in their responses to queries about delicate issues had to be tackled with utmost care and discretion.

The research exercise began with a survey of the existing literature and a pilot study in the selected villages. All issues and subjects and information relating to the adolescent girls were explored. The fact that these girls are a part of a closely knit family structure situated in the village environment, which is bound by its traditions and limitations made it essential to understand them in their social context. Thus, for instance, their problems and needs regarding education were analysed both in terms of their parents' attitude towards education plus the availability or non-availability of educational facilities in the village infrastructure.

The data was collected in relation to the adolescent girl at different levels:

a) at the level of the village
b) from the available population of adolescent girls
c) the adolescent girl herself, and
d) the parents of the adolescent girl

For each of these, therefore, a questionnaire was prepared. The issues identified for exploring her problems and needs are in the context of:

a) her education
b) work pattern
c) leisure
d) marriage
e) general awareness about health and hygiene and her health status
f) her wishes and aspirations
g) problems specific to the girl

Thus, on education for example questions were asked about her educational status. In case she is school-going, where, when and how she goes to school? What interests her at school? Does she perceive any benefits of education? If she does, what are they? In case she is not going to school, what is the reason? It was essential to clearly distinguish between the problems of the girl herself (viz. she does not feel like going to the school); the problems perceived in relation to her family (viz. she is the eldest in the sibling hierarchy, therefore, she has to work at home) and the problems relating to infrastructural facilities in her village (viz. lack of a girls' school in the village).

The pre-testing for data collection was initially done with the help of a questionnaire with close-ended questions. It was found that the girl responded in the affirmative to most of such questions. Thus, for instance, when asked "what do you do in case you get some free time?", she would say 'yes' to all the listed activities. It became quite difficult to decipher what she actually did, perceived and wished. The questions, therefore, were changed to open-ended ones to elicit the desired information from the girls.

Progress and Problems of Data Collection

To conduct a pilot survey our research team on its initial visit to the selected villages encountered both positive and negative responses of the villagers. In most of the villages we were perceived as outsiders coming from urban centres, who invariably disturb the harmony of the village system. We were frequently questioned about our age and marital status. We were seen as paid employees of the government who were whiling away our time. It was difficult for the villagers to understand why we had left our 'comfortable' city-dwellings and gone to study their life in the village. Some of them were suspicious of our motives, whereas, others showed enthusiasm for the proposed project. However, whatever their private feelings could have been - varying from being amused, anxious, irritated or enthusiastic, the rural people received us well.

In the initial stages of data collection, the research investigators had to make individual contact with the help of the local volunteer to establish rapport with the subjects. Our strategy to equip the research team with one trained researcher and one young woman volunteer from the villages under study proved to be effective in this context. Reaching the villages daily for them, specially in the summer and rainy season proved to be quite an ardous task as there was a transport problem. At times no vehicle would be available for commuting to and fro from the village and, indeed, no *pucca* roads existed in several villages.

The research investigators and volunteers initially had problems of mobility in the villages as they belonged to a certain caste. (If they were from an upper caste, their family members raised objections to their visiting the lower-caste houses and vice-versa).

The research team interviewed the adolescent girl and her parents simultaneously. A minimum of three hours were spent on each session. Since many of the questions were open-ended, it was often necessary to interview the subject a second time to elicit detailed information. This was necessary because the girls felt hesitant and inhibited while answering certain questions.

Initially, the parents were reluctant to answer questions but were eager to know what kind of programme was being planned for their daughters and when it would begin. The response to some of our questions was quite critical and sometimes even antagonistic. It had an element of fatalism, on the one hand, and anxious expectations on the other. Whatever may be the case, most of them expected a grand programme to emerge instantly out of this kind of exercise. The mothers were not very happy because they considered this exercise as being time-consuming and upsetting their household work schedule. Further, the nature of certain questions pertaining to bodily functions, childbirth and marriage evoked a sharp reaction from them as having an adverse effect on their daughters.

Coming down to the adolescent girls, the investigators faced different sets of problems. Communication with girls of the age group twelve and above was relatively easier than with the age group of ten to twelve, as they were less inhibited and more responsive. The 10-12 age group girls, were both shy and ignorant of the issues surrounding which the questions were to be asked. They were also least exposed to information either informally through social interaction or formally through educational media. The research team had to wait for the school going girls as they were unavailable in the forenoon. Often they had to wait for the girl to finish the task at hand, both in the house or out in the fields. Usually the girls were shy about responding to questions relating to menstruation, marriage, childbirth and individual problems. The presence of the mother made it even more difficult as sometimes in the middle of the conversation, she would take away the girl on the pretext of the household work or by vigilantly interfering in the process of interview.

Group Discussion

Early in the planning phase of the project itself we had visualised the importance and role of group discussion with the interviewees, so as to bring out information individual interviewees may have hesitated to give. This could be so as they may be ignorant of or afraid of giving information due to nervousness, or owing to partial awareness. It was also necessary to cross-check the individual responses.

This led us to train the investigators and field volunteer staff on the mode of discussion and objectives of the study. Our experts conducted three briefing sessions in each of the States.

Equipped with the advantage of being residents of the locality/region and proficiency in the local language and dialect, these field staff volunteers (all girls) were further instructed on the objectives of the study, the reasons for the structuring of the questionnaire, the possible gaps in information collected through the questionnaire method, the need to draw out the interviewees, the way to develop rapport with the village girls and households, how to encourage them to shed inhibitions, and individually and collectively complementing the information required through cross questioning, offering defensive interpretations to responses, mutual self correction and checking of responses, etc. The volunteers were also briefed about organising, style and methods of conducting group discussions, their role as prompters and invisible regulators of the trend of discussions.

This painstaking effort of training and briefing the volunteer investigators paid rich dividends in the quality of information we gathered. Further, we could cross check, and were successful in arousing full participation of the respondents, etc.

In order to supplement the acquired information through the questionnaire, group discussions were organised in all the villages. The aim of this was to observe the group behaviour pattern of the selected girls and attempt to identify future volunteers and leaders. Starting with a general introduction, information was sought at different levels:

a) reaction to the questionnaire: what did the girls think about it and how did they feel answering certain questions and did it, in any way, give them new information?
b) what is the level of information of these girls and their exposure to mass media
c) problems of the girl - her reality and how she perceives this reality. Here problems were seen in three contexts: (i) village, (ii) family, (iii) girl herself
d) needs of the girl
e) her aspirations - what were her aspirations and how could she fulfil them; what was her level of information regarding the mode of fulfilling those aspirations
f) what did the girl wish to do in life

Certain other issues on which information was sought through group discussions were:

a) personal cleanliness of the adolescent girls (with special focus on the type/kind of water available and used)

b) information on who determined the sex preference of the child
c) vaccination of the child, why the vaccination, what is it for
d) special focus on what the girls wished to do in case centres were opened in their villages
e) girl's physiology and bodily functions: specially menstruation, and how the girls viewed it
f) her self-image and concept of personhood
g) discrimination, beatings, fasts and acts of self-denial
h) extent of exposure to media

There were two significant problems in organising the group discussions in the villages. Firstly, it was regarding the availability of the girls owing to the fact that some of them were school-going and others were not. Those staying at home were, at times, busy doing domestic work or working in the fields. Therefore, one had to choose a time when the majority of the girls would be available. Secondly, assembling them as a group under the same roof was problematic. In the context of the caste structure in the village, at times, lower-caste girls were hesitant to either join or participate in the group discussion in the presence of the upper caste girls. Sometimes, they were even physically segregated. For instance, in Noh and Nogayan/Bharatpur (Rajasthan), Heerapur (Jaunpur) (U.P.) girls from the lower caste sat as a separate group. Once these girls were organised as a group, there were problems of communication. The girls were quite hesitant to respond to certain sets of questions. For instance, questions regarding menstruation and child-birth were treated as being dirty and were, therefore, evaded. This was so even regarding questions on personal problems, presumably because of the fear that it might become a subject of public gossip in the village. However, in all the villages, the girls were very enthusiastic about singing and dancing as a group.

Like other studies, ours too was hampered by constraints of time. We had just nine months at hand to analyse and understand the problems and needs of a considerably large sample size. According to Robert Chambers, the direct rural experience of most urban based outsiders is limited to the brief and hurried visit from urban centres of "rural development tourism". In our study, in order to minimize and to a large extent overcome this problem, we selected village women/girl volunteers to help the trained research investigators in the data-collection process. This enabled us to maintain the continuity over time. Moreover, our study conducted in the remote villages of Jaunpur and some in Bharatpur does not suffer from the spatial and seasonal biases. This is so because we selected villages even if they were not approachable. And, in fact, it was during the summer and rainy season that we initiated the process of data-collection, even though accessibility to the villages is more difficult and working conditions are not so favourable during this period.

Despite the problems and difficulties encountered we were successful in collecting the desired information. Cross-checking of this information through the group discussions helped in comprehending the specificities of a rural young girl's life. The cooperation of the village community made the task somewhat easier. Our own perceptions and insights through homework were of immense help in understanding the life of these girls. An in-depth analysis of their problems and needs, based on the collected information and experience follows in the subsequent sections.

Chapter Three

Village Profile

The problems and needs of adolescent girls cannot be identified and understood in isolation from their social context. The development of the village infrastructure has even had a bearing on their life - pattern.

Socio-Demographic Profile of the Villages

The semi-urban villages of Delhi and Bharatpur are quite easily approachable unlike the Jaunpur villages, most of which do not have a *pucca* road leading upto them.

Rangpuri and Kishangarh are situated in South Delhi, and have an area of three hundred bigas each. The approximate population of these villages is eight thousand and five thousand respectively. About six hundred families live in Rangpuri and three hundred and fifty in the village of Kishangarh.

Both the villages are surrounded by jungles. The land around Rangpuri is fertile, whereas around Kishangarh it is barren.

Table 3.1: Socio-demographic Profile of the Villages

Name of village	Area	Population	Type of soil/land
DELHI			
Rangpuri	300 bigas	8000	fertile
Kishangarh	300 "	5000	barren
RAJASTHAN			
Malahe	3805 "	2800	Chikni-domat and sandy

Sewar	6185 "	5683	"
Malipura	5285 "	3000	"
Noh	753 "	975	"
Noganya	360 "	2500	"
Peepla	8500 "	4500	"
UTTAR PRADESH			
Heerapur	1103 "	500	fertile
Ramnagar	800 "	2500	fertile
Banspha	80 "	1300	fertile
Baghela	400 "	1500	fertile

Out of the six villages of Bharatpur district in Rajasthan, Sewar is the largest in terms of its area and population and Noh the smallest. Whereas, Malahe, Malipura and Sewar are situated in the southwest of Bharatpur, Noganya and Peepla are in the Northwest. Sewar being the largest village, has many facilities which are utilised by Malahe and Malipura as well.

The villages in Jaunpur district in Uttar Pradesh form a cluster of villages that are about 80 km. from Varanasi. There is no 'pucca' road leading upto these villages. The nearest is upto Gulzarganj which is situated at a distance of 8 km. from these villages. The land around these villages is reasonably fertile. Whereas some areas are irrigated, the others are not.

Socio-Economic Profile of Residents

In our study, we selected girls belonging to different sections in each village; they were classified into upper, middle and lower castes. Girls between the age group of 10-16 years were chosen proportionally from each caste. Table 3.2 gives information on the caste distribution, family type, occupational and educational status of villagers in different areas. Here the classification of the respondents by caste status is although arbitrary, based on conventional standards prevalent in the villages.

Table 3.2: Socio-economic Profile of Residents

Name of Village	Approx. No. of families	Type of families	Major occupation	Educational status	Available population of girls between 10-16 years
DELHI					
Rangpuri	600	more nuclear	servicemen labourers, farmers, porters	upper caste educated	292
Kishangarh	350	more nuclear	barbers, washermen, etc.	very few from middle & lower castes are educated	158
RAJASTHAN					
Malahe	312	more joint	farmers, carpenters	most upper caste people are educated	153
Sewar	486	more nuclear	dairy-farming animal husbandry, govt. jobs, etc.		207
Malipura	208	more nuclear	"		88
Noh	184	more joint	"		83
Noganya	207	more nuclear	"		92
Peepla	378	more nuclear	"		162
UTTAR PRADESH					
Heerapur	170	more joint	farming, carpenters, barbers, blacksmiths, etc.	only 113 of population is literate	85
Ramnagar	340	more joint			152
Banspha	139	more joint			68
Baghela	171	more joint			85

In the villages around Delhi, there are more nuclear families than joint. Similarly in Rajasthan, except Malahe and Noh, the number of nuclear families exceeds that of the joint ones. In Jaunpur, however, there are more joint families. This may indicate the influence of the nearby city centres on the former villages in terms of breaking up of a large family unit into smaller ones.

Although the major occupation of the villagers varies, it is predominantly agricultural activity. The other avenues of work open to people are dairy farming, animal husbandry, carpentry, masonry, teaching, etc. Some villagers are employed in government offices.

Different caste groups exist in each village. However, there is a dominance of one caste or the other in almost all the villages. Thus, whereas Jats are dominant in Kishangarh at Delhi, in Jaunpur villages there is a predominant Rajput population. Moreover, in all the three areas, upper caste people are more educated than the middle and lower castes. In fact, very few people among lower castes are educated.

Section 2

The problems regarding the availability of the infrastructural facilities and their relationship to our subject of study were looked into at two levels: those which concerned the village at large and those which concerned the girls in particular. Thus, facilities regarding education, health, drinking water, women's programmes, availability of TV, newspapers, etc. were surveyed in relation to the young girls.

Education

The educational status and opportunities available to the girls in the villages were directly related to either certain infrastructural constraints or some social constraints and in some cases both. Thus, for instance, in some villages girls were not going to the school because there was no school in the village, whereas in others, despite the presence of the school, parents were not sending their daughters to the school because it was co-educational. In such villages most of the girls dropped out of school at the primary level. The absence of a girl's school at the secondary level in the village, thus reinforced the parents' aversal to educating their daughters.

Table 3.3: Educational Facilities in the Villages

Name of Village	No. of primary schools	No. of secondary schools	No. of higher secondary schools
DELHI			
Rangpuri	2	-	-
Kishangarh	1	-	-
RAJASTHAN			
Malahe	1	-	-
Malipura	1	-	-
Sewar	5	2	1
Noh	1	-	-
Noganya	1	-	-
Peepla	2	1	1
UTTAR PRADESH			
Heerapur	-	-	-
Ramnagar	1	-	-
Banspha	1	-	-
Baghela	-	-	-

Whereas Heerapur and Baghela in Jaunpur do not have a school at all, the rest have at least a primary school. Only Sewar and Peepla in Bharatpur have secondary and higher secondary schools as well. The absence of a girls' school in Malahe and Noh at Bharatpur prevents the girls from being educated as the parents feel their daughters will get spoilt in a co-educational school. Moreover, the schools being situated at a distance from the village also acts as a deterrent. In Delhi, for instance, the higher secondary school is situated at a distance from the villages. (In Mehrauli, 2 miles away from Kishangarh and at Mahipalpur, 4 miles away from Rangpuri). Many girls said that they are not allowed to go to the school because parents worry about their safety. They complained of lack of transport to the school as being a major problem. Similarly, girls at Malipura in Bharatpur said that their parents do not allow them to attend the Higher Secondary School at Sewar far from the village, because of the fear of misbehaviour by others on the way.

Wherever the schools do exist, they are not well equipped. The girls complained of lack of drinking water facilities, libraries, science laboratories and unhygenic conditions, etc. and also about teachers' carelessness and lack of interest in teaching.

Health

The availability of medical facilities was seen in relation to the health status of the girls. They were observed not merely in terms of the access which the girls have or do not have to them but also in relation to their level of information about these facilities.

Table 3.4: Health Care Facilities in the Villages

Name of village	Primary Health Centre	Maternity Home	Private practi- tioners	Hakims Ojhas, Vaidya, etc.
DELHI				
Rangpuri	-	-	2	-
Kishangarh	1	-	15	-
RAJASTHAN				
Malahe	1	-	2	-
Malipura	-	-	-	-
Sewar	1	1 (Pvt.)	1	6
Noh	-	-	-	3
Noganya	-	-	-	-
Peepla	1	-	-	3
UTTAR PRADESH				
Heerapur	-	-	-	-
Ramnagar	-	-	-	1
Banspha	-	-	-	-
Baghela	-	-	-	-

The availability of medical facilities is quite poor in almost all the villages. They are particularly insufficient in the interior villages at Jaunpur, where only Ramnagar has a Hakim.

The villagers resort to their domestic-remedies in case of emergencies as well as for common ailments. The villagers are infected with many diseases, particularly the water-borne ones. None of the villages has a proper drainage system. The drains are kuccha and open. There is waterlogging and cesspools across the villages. The unhygienic and unhealthy conditions thus provide ideal breeding grounds for the vectors and parasites of endemic diseases like malaria, diarrhoea and jaundice.

There is acute shortage of potable water, especially at times of unprecedented drought. The situation was particularly acute as in villages of Rajasthan. This acute shortage of water, felt more severely in summer, forces the women and children, especially the girls to spend a great deal of their working time in fetching water. The shortage of water affects cleanliness, as they cannot afford to wash themselves properly every day and keep their surroundings clean.

Similarly shortage of fuel for cooking, and fodder for the cattle, affects these girls as they are the ones who are entrusted with the task of collecting fuel wood from nearby bushes and forests, and feeding/grazing the cattle. This takes away another great part of their waking hours.

In addition, there is lack of proper toilet facilities, particularly for women. In Jaunpur villages, for instance, girls complained of water-logging during the monsoons which hampered defecation. Our research investigators from this area informed that many a women suffer from leukeoria. In the absence of a lady doctor in the village, they refuse to go to a male doctor for treatment.

Although girls are quite well informed about health issues in those villages, in very few cases is this information put to use. Thus, whereas girls know about most of the prevalent diseases in their villages, very few know about their cause or cure. The school-going girls from villages near cities and having access to such sources of information as the radio, TV, newspapers, magazine, etc. are better informed on such issues. Those exposed in such manner, especially the ones who are informed through media or in the school environment, have heard of names of different diseases, sometimes even means to prevent them through immunisation. They are also in a better position regarding the availability and utilization of health facilities unlike the girls from very interior villages who neither have the information, either through education and social interaction or through media like TV, nor have access to facilities. This overall non-exposure to vital information regarding health, common diseases, sanitation, personal and social hygiene, prevention of various diseases through vaccination, oral rehydration therapy, etc. is responsible for their generally poor health, disease proneness and illness rate. Of course, the urgent need for providing hospitals, sanitation, clean drinking water and other basic facilities cannot be overlooked.

Natural Resources/Asset Structure

The availability of such resources as drinking water, firewood, etc. was assessed keeping in mind the fact that fetching water and collecting firewood are two necessary tasks undertaken by young girls in the villages. The absence of taps and running water in the village puts an additional burden of fetching drinking water from distant sources, either wells, ponds or taps.

Table 3.5: Natural Resources/Asset Structure of Villages

Area	Source of water	Type of water
Delhi	Tap, handpump, well	Potable
Bharatpur	Well, pond and in some villages tap	barely potable
Jaunpur	Well, handpump, and ponds	potable

The problem of drinking water is particularly acute in the villages of Rajasthan. Girls spend considerable period of time in fetching water. Even if the houses have taps, the task of filling and storing water is done by young girls.

Only a negligible number of houses in these villages have a solar cooker, firewood is the chief source of fuel. Its collection in generally done by girls. Moreover, not just its collection but even cooking on a slow fire is a tedious task. Added to this the girls complained of the harmful effects of smoke on their eyes and the problem of blackened and dirty walls. In the villages in Delhi, however, stoves and gas burners are used which saves them from the trouble of firewood collection.

Programmes for Women and Employment Opportunities

Viewing this girl as a future worker, employment opportunities for her as a woman and existing programmes for women in the villages were looked into. Although some programmes for women have been organised in a few villages, like TRYSEM and Adult Education courses in Sewar, none of the villages has any specific programmes for young girls. Some non-governmental agencies have been working in these villages to conscientize the female population. Although different avenues of work like weaving, stitching, knitting, agricultural work, wage labour, etc. are open to women in these areas, women at large confine themselves to household tasks. For the young girls in these villages, there are very limited sources of information regarding possible employment in the future. Thus, even though some of the girls from Delhi villages expressed the desire to be nurses, doctors, teachers, etc, they, however, did not know about relevant courses on each of these.

Apart from these particular areas, information was sought about the availability of other facilities like banking, post and telegraph, police thana, community centre, panchayat ghar, electricity, etc. The presence of radio, television, magazines, etc, was viewed in connection with the exposure to mass media and its possible influence on the general awareness and level of information of the girl. Although, except for Jaunpur, most of the villages had at least one television set, it must not be seen as an adequate source of information dissemination and entertainment because it is not available to a significant section of the population, since these TV sets were privately owned.

In conclusion, we may say that although, almost all the villages are poorly equipped with various facilities, the problem is particularly acute in the interior villages. The girls in these interior villages are doubly disadvantaged because of social constraints and negative attitudes coupled with the absence of basic infrastructural facilities.

Chapter Four

Growing Up in Indian Villages

Socio-Demographic Profile of the Young Girls

Age of the Rural Young Girls

The age group covered in our study between 10 to 16 years as shown below:

Table 4.1: Age Distribution[1]

Age group	No. of girls	Percentage
No response	6	1.50
10-12	46	11.50
12-14	85	21.25
14-16	263	65.75
Total	**400**	**100.00**

* Girls who did not respond when asked may be because they did not know their age.

11.5 per cent girls are from the age group 10-12 years, 21.25 per cent from 12-14 years and 65.75 per cent from 14-16 years. 1.5 per cent girls are those who appeared to be of the age under study but did not respond to the question on age.

Religion and Caste of Rural Young Girls

In our sample, we have rural young girls belonging to the Hindu and

Muslim communities. We did not come across any Sikh, Christian, Jain or Buddhist young girls of the age groups under consideration in the selected villages. Here the classification by caste status is based on conventional criteria recognized by the villagers, especially in the case of assigning upper, middle or lower status.

Table 4.2 : Religion/Caste Distribution of young girls

Caste/Religion	No. of girls	Percentage
No response	4	1.0
Upper Caste	198	49.5
Intermediate	104	26.0
Lower	87	21.75
Muslims	7	1.75
Total	**400**	**100.00**

Note:
The classification of different castes into upper, middle and lower castes is arbitrary, but based on the accepted traditions of the village. Interestingly, the respondents themselves agreed on the prevalent classification. Accordingly, Brahmins, Rajputs, Kshatriyas, Vaisyas, and Banias were regarded by them as belonging to the Upper Castes. Ahirs, Yadavas, Jats, Kurmis and Gujjars as belonging to Middle Castes and Mallahs, Badais, Telis, Nais, Chamars, Passis, Gaderias, Bhangis, Lohars, Khatiks and many of their subsects as belonging to lower castes. Mostly, this division is based on their professions and the work they do (*Karma*) rather than *Dharma*.

1.75 per cent girls are Muslims and 97.25 are Hindus. Out of the latter, 49.5 per cent are from Upper Castes, 26 per cent from Middle Castes and 21.75 from Lower Castes. 1 per cent of the girls did not respond to the question on caste.

Educational Profiles

Our sample is heterogenous, consisting of both educated and uneducated girls.

Whereas 15.75 per cent girls did not respond to the question about their educational status, 18 per cent admitted to being uneducated; 21.25 per cent were educated upto primary, 18.75 per cent upto middle and 18.75 upto secondary. 7.5 per cent girls are educated upto higher secondary. Thus there were 265 girls (66.5 percent

Table 4.3: Educational Profiles of the Girls

Level of education	No. of girls	Percentage
No response	63	15.75
Uneducated	72	18.00
Upto Primary School	85	21.25
Upto Middle School	75	18.75
Upto Secondary School	75	18.75
Upto Higher Secondary	30	7.50
Total	**400**	**100.00**

of the total number) who have had some level of education. This, of course does not take into account those who did not respond to the question on educational status.

The category of educated girls (total 265 or 66.5 per cent) include both the school going and the drop-outs, and excludes those who did not respond to the question on educational status.

Table 4.4: Educational Status of the Girls

Response	No. of girls	Percentage
School going	192	72.45
Drop-outs	73	27.55
Total educated	**265**	**100.00**

Out of the total number of girls in our sample 33.75 per cent have never been to the school. (This figure includes those who did not respond to the question on educational status and is therefore admittedly somewhat arbitrary. Out of the total of 265 or 66.25 per cent of girls who have been to school 27.55 per cent or 73 have dropped out. This constitutes about 18.25 per cent of the total example, though this figure may be higher if we include those who did not respond to the question, as high as 34 per cent. The school going girls joined school at different age levels.

Table 4.5: School-going Girls -- Age-wise

Age of joining school	No. of girls	Percentage
Not certain or did not want to respond	47	24.47
4 years	29	15.12
5 years	108	26.25
6 years	6	3.12
7 years	2	1.04
Total	**192**	**100.00**

A majority of the 56.25 per cent school-going girls joined school at the age of five. A very small percentage of 3.12 and 1.04 joined at the age of 6 and 7 years respectively. 24.47 per cent did not know the age at which they joined school and, therefore, did not respond. In our sample, thus, the otherwise widespread phenomenon of sending girls late to school does not hold true.

Marital Status

That the phenomenon of early marriage still exists was quite evident in our sample. Although 78.25 per cent girls in our sample are unmarried the fact of the remaining 21.75 per cent girls from this age group being married is alarming.

Table 4.6: Distribution of Sample Showing Marital Status

Marital Status	No. of girls	Percentage
Unmarried (total)	(313)	(78.25)
Delhi	60	15.00
Bharatpur	180	45.00
Jaunpur	73	18.25
Married (total)	(87)	(21.75)
Delhi	10	2.50
Bharatpur	18	4.50
Jaunpur	59	14.75
Total	**400**	**100.00**

The married girls were married at different ages. Out of 87 girls, 10.34 per cent got married when they were between 8-10 years of age. 32.18 per cent got married between 10-12 years and 20.68 between 12-14 years. 36.80 got married at the age of 14-16 years.

Table 4.7: Distribution of Sample indicating Age at Marriage

Age at marriage	No. of girls	Percentage
8-10 years	9	10.34
10-12 years	28	32.19
12-14 years	18	20.68
14-16 years	32	36.80
Total	**87**	**100.00**

Family Type, Size and their Position in Sibling Hierarchy

The joint family system is still prevalent in our society, and the majority of the girls came from joint families. However, some came from nuclear families and female-headed households as well.

Table 4.8: Family Type of the Girls

Type of families	No. of families	Percentage
No response	18	4.5
Nuclear (N)	152	38.0
Joint (J)	212	53.0
Female-headed (N)	7	1.75
Female-headed (J)	11	2.75
Total	**400**	**100.00**

Note:

1. Here the term female-headed household is used for those families which have no male spouse or partner present at any time, i.e. households headed by single mothers, divorcees, widows or separated women, from which the male spouse or partner is temporarily absent or present but disabled, unemployed and unable to contribute to family income. Nuclear families are those in which the husband or wife or both control and contribute to the family finances, and others living with them, if any are only adjunct residents sharing accommodation, food and helping in work on the basis of obliga-

tions of relationships. Joint families are those where apart from parents, a number of male or female or both members contribute to finances, the eldest making decisions and controlling affairs.

2. The high number in the no response group is due to the fact that, they were either coming from families where there is no clear-cut and rigid definition of the family type was applicable or they were not certain about the definition.

53 pei cent girls are from joint families, 38 per cent are from nuclear and 4.5 per cent from female-headed households. The average family size is quite large with majority having 8-12 members. 48.75 per cent families have 8-12 members and 44.5 per cent have 4-8 members. Some which are joint families, have 12-14 (2 per cent) and even more than 12 members (1 per cent), only 2 per cent families have just 1-4 members.

Table 4.9: Number of Siblings in Respondents' Household

No. of siblings	No. of families	Percentage
No response	3	0.75
Only child	9	2.25
Two	5	1.25
Three	31	7.75
Four	123	30.75
Five	195	48.75
Six	26	6.05
Seven	8	2.00
Total	**400**	**100.00**

Note:

1. Household here is defined as family of persons living under one roof, sharing food and incomes, and jointly contributing to the family finances. It is distinct from family in the sense that it is more nuclear than the latter which may not be living in the same premises, and may be cooking separately and having separate finances incomes and control over incomes. Yet, the social bondage may be strong.

30.75 per cent respondents had in their household four siblings, 48.75 per cent had five siblings, 6.5 had six and 21 had 7. Only 2.25 per cent or 9 respondents had one child while only 1.25 per cent had two. 0.75 per cent respondents did not respond.

The majority of the rural young girls in our sample were the eldest in the sibling hierarchy.

Table 4.10: Position of Respondents in Sibling Hierarchy

Position in sibling hierarchy	No. of girls	Percentage
No response	4	1.0
First child	209	52.25
Second child	86	21.50
Third child	85	21.25
Fourth child	16	4.00
Total	**400**	**100.00**

52.25 per cent of the girls in our sample were the eldest child whereas 21.50 per cent were second and 21.25 the third child. Only 4 per cent were the fourth child. This also may reflect the age status of the parents. Thus, in the case of the fourth children, the parents were relatively aged as compared to the next categories of 21.25, 21.50 and 52.25 per cent in order. It indicates that in most of the cases, the parents were young adults who were married about 8 to 18 years earlier.

Profile of Young Girls

What does it mean to be a girl in an Indian rural situation? At what stage in her life does a girl become conscious of the constraints under which she has to live of the discrimination between male and female children? When and how does she learn the content of roles accorded to her? What are the different mechanisms and structures through which she internalises the given roles? How does she develop and form an image of herself? What notion of femaleness does she have? - i.e. "... how are women produced as gendered subjects".[1] Our study on problems and needs of adolescent girls in rural areas addresses itself to such and related questions.

The process of growing up as a female in the Indian rural situation in a complex one. Unlike the urban situation where we can find a clearly demarcated stage of adolescence which gives ample time and space for growth between child-hood and adulthood, in our study we have found that in the rural context such a stage is missing.

With the onset of puberty the girl-child is immediately transformed into a women. In our sample, the average age at menstruation is 14 years. It marks a period of sharp discontinuity in the girl's life and changes in her life pattern can be clearly demarcated between the pre-pubertal and post-pubertal phases.

What are these changes? In many Indian languages menstruation is likened to the process at flowering or blossoming -- a necessary stage before fruit can appear. References to her full-grown body: *'Ladki Badi Ho Gayi Hai'*, ('The girl is grown up now'), *'Jawan Ho Gayi Hai'*, *'Sayani Ho Gayi Hai'* (She is young, she is mature), etc, express the fact of her changed status. Expressions such as her 'body is full', 'it is ripe', 'it is ready', are common. Menstruation brings with it two things simultaneously - not merely the capacity for full sexual life but the related capacity to reproduce. The girl, however, has no independent authority to exercise either. It is her father's responsibility to get her married off. The period, between puberty and marriage is crucial and several restrictions are put on the girl. These are in the context of: (a) the prevalence of the notion of 'impurity' or 'being impure' attached to a menstruating girl. This is a tradition sanctified from Vedic times in Indian society which forbids menstruating women from coming into contact with others in the house, from entering the kitchen, prayer rooms, etc. and (b) her emergent sexuality and consequently the problem of 'protecting' her virginity -- keeping her safe and secure. Obviously, the purpose is to keep a check on promiscuity.

Self-Perception of Menstruating Girl: Image of an Impure Women:
In our study, the perception of a menstruating girl as being impure and the subsequent justification of the restrictions put on her comes out quite strongly. The idea that a woman is impure when menstruating finds expression firstly in the *Brahmanas* (Shastri, 1954). The later Hindu laws too reiterate this idea. That their monthly period or the menstrual flow is a mark of sin has been widely accepted in the Hindu society from Vedic times, in its sacred scriptures and daily practice.[2]

The girls when asked about menstruation were shy to answer as they treated it as something 'dirty' and private. Restrictions within the household vary from not being allowed to do certain domestic and extra domestic tasks to religious tasks. Thus, for instance, girls are not allowed to cook food, touch the drinking-water vessel, enter the *pooja sthala* - in case of married girls not wear *sindoor*, etc.

Table 4.11: Levels of Self Perception of Menstruating Girls

Response	10-12	12-14	14-16	Total	Percentage
No response	42	50	113	215	53.75
No restriction	2	4	18	24	6.00
No allowed to touch water	1	10	55	66	16.05
Not allowed to cook food	1	1	78	80	20.00
Not allowed to enter pooja sthala	1	2	4	7	1.75
Not allowed to go out	0	0	1	1	0.25
Not allowed to do any household work	0	2	5	7	1.75

Table 4.12: Restrictions during the Menstruation

Response	Number	Percentage
Didn't respond	215	53.75
Yes, restriction	161	40.25
No restriction	24	6.00
Total	**400**	**100.00**

Thus, whereas 53.75 per cent did not respond, 40.25 per cent did specify some form of restriction and only 6 per cent said there were no restrictions. Out of those who did not respond, some girls mostly from the age-group 10-12, and the number of girls in this cohort is very high, did so because they haven't reached puberty yet. But those from the other age groups (particularly those from 14-16 years) did so because they felt shy and hesitant to talk about it. They treated themselves as 'impure' and 'dirty' while menstruating. Most of the girls who said there are restrictions are from upper caste (80.12). However, the practice is operative even among middle (11.28) and lower (8.60) castes. Out of the almost negligible but significant number who said there were no restrictions, 54.16 came from middle castes.

It is pertinent to emphasize that such customs which treat the girls as untouchables and the accompanying notion of a 'periodical impurity' has resulted in their low self-perception of themselves and a poor self-image - the girls look at themselves as being impure, and hence inferior and accept the restrictions as being natural without questioning them.

On the other hand, and in contrast to the notion of impurity attached to a menstruating girl, a pre-pubertal girl is viewed as being endowed with an intrinsic purity. She is treated as a manifestation of 'Devi'. This is amply illustrated by an interesting custom we came across in the villages around Bharatpur in Rajasthan. This year (1987), in the wake of acute drought, pre-pubertal girls in different villages embarked on a long fast at the fields to invoke the blessings of the rain-god, Indra. These girls are treated as 'Devi-matas' and as a mark of distinction wear a white piece of cloth around their hair which is tied in a top-knot. In case rain followed their fasting, these girls were taken on a pilgrimage to one of the Tirath Sthalas (like Haridwara, Varanasi, etc.) to mark their supernatural powers. In the eastern U.P. region there is a prevalent practice of 'Kumari Pujah'. Pre-pubertal girls are invited to a feast and given gifts on this occasion. The point which needs to be underscored here is that the purity and the consequent privileged status of a girl in the pre-pubertal stage contrasts acutely with her puberty and post-pubertal status. This demarcation defines the latter phase with remarkable clarity. The fact remains that such practices do result in the impairment of the physical and mental growth of these girls. We are all aware that even a moderate growth retardation results in lowered stamina and has negative implications for the productivity and learning ability.

Controls on Her Sexuality and Mobility

Further, in view of her emergent sexuality, the restrictions on her mobility extend quite fastidiously outside the house-premises too. The time, 'when' and the place 'where' they can go are decided by their parents. Most of the girls can't venture out alone they must be accompanied by someone, usually the father or brother -- more importantly a male member of the family. None of them can stay outside once it gets dark. Most of the school-going girls in our sample either go in groups or are accompanied by a family member. In fact, in Noh (at Bharatpur) a girl, Bhoodevi has discontinued schooling because there is no one to accompany her. Around sixty-six (26.5 per cent) school-going girls (ie. those who have either been to the school or are still going) and 135 (33.75 per cent) non-school-going gave the following response.

Table 4.13: Response of the School-going Girls

Response	10-12	13-14	14-16	Total	Percentage
No response	15	30	44	89	33.60
Relatives accompany	6	2	13	21	7.92
Friends	12	14	45	71	26.79
Nobody	7	12	65	84	31.69
				265	**100.00**

Table 4.14: Responses of the Non-school Going Girls

Response	Percentage
Can go out like brothers	13.0
Can go only to certain places	19.5
Allowed if being accompanied	22.0
Can't go out like brothers	45.5
	100.00

When asked if they could go out as freely as their brothers, most said they could not.

Only 13.0 per cent girls could go out like their brothers did. 45.5 per cent said they could not. 41.5 qualified their answers : 19.5 could go only to certain places and 22.0 only if they were being accompanied. It is amply clear that parents don't allow their daughters to move around freely as they treat it as a security risk.

The constraints are therefore, set out in the context of specific notions of time and space. "... her body almost shrinking, a girl is expected to create space for herself in places full of strangers". Moreover, not only are girls burdened with a variety of do's and don'ts in many cases the girls are asked to discontinue studies once they attain puberty, because now they are 'grown-ups'. In our sample, although the majority of the school-going girls joined school at the age of five to six years, many dropped out of school after class IX or X which is just a year or two after reaching puberty (14-16) years. The low percentage of 22.9 per cent at class VIII and 19.27 per cent in class IX, of the total number of school-going girls, for example, is indicative of the restrictions associated with the onset of puberty.

Often a feeling of genuine fear on the part of the parents about the girl's security coupled with a growing worry and doubt that more education and freedom would 'spoil' their daughters, acts as a deterrent. Moreover, parents do not see any benefit of such education as they feel that their daughters would get married and go to their *sasural* -- they must, therefore, be trained in household work rather than have money wasted on their education.

The onset of puberty and the consequent restrictions are, thus, accompanied by the assigning of new roles to the girl. She is no longer a child but grown-up and is expected to perform various tasks. The girl not only shares her mothers' workload, but in some cases, completely absolves her of the household responsibilities so that the mother can work in the fields. It is interesting to see that whereas a pre-pubertal girl performs many tasks outside the house, the post-pubertal girl is confined to the tasks inside the house. "Beginning with assistance in cooking and other kitchen work, serving of food, caring for younger siblings, preparing for worship of family deities, and looking after the aged, girls learn to take over some of the responsibilities themselves."[3]

Thus the social attitude towards the young girl is not necessarily positive most of the time. Not getting an adequate share of the nutritional resources, lack of knowledge on health issues, no scientific education on matters of sex and family planning, lack of physical training, lack of health care and knowledge of health care, no access to proper environmental hygiene along with the cultural biases involved in the upbringing of these girls all combine to inculcate a low self-image in them. And it also leads to malnourished and under developed bodies. Even though, many of these girls may look healthy but the amount of work-load which they have in terms of studying, washing clothes, cleaning, cooking, looking after cattle, collecting water and firewood besides taking care of their siblings, is time-consuming and leaves no room for relaxation. Thus, discrimination in the quantity and quality of their food-share, not having a particularly strong body, having a low self-image, lack of information and the burden of being over worked all go hand in hand in creating, a situation for girls that is not conducive at all to their proper personality development.

Chapter Five

Marrying them Young

"In the mythological formulations, female is seen as complementing the male, to create. She is necessary to nurture man's need and without him life is not possible. Symbolically too, the religious text refer to her as 'Ardhanagini' - His half body, a part of man". This religious belief has far reaching bearing on the minds of people in rural India towards the reproductive roles of women. Marriage is the sole institution sanctioned for procreation. This deep-rooted religious understanding is a widely accepted social norm in rural India. Also, the reproductive functions of women through marriage is valued in term of continuity of the family lineage. It is seen as the duty of woman to perpetuate her race and to continue her life as a loyal and chaste wife. The sole objective set up before a growing girl is thus to get married and to procreate, preferably a son who will continue the family lineage. There is also a lot of emphasis on control of female sexuality. This is done through handing her over from father's control to her husband's.

Absolute control of the sexually active women is maintained by imposing rigid restrictions on her from the moment she attains maturity or even puberty and menarche. With the onset of menstruation, the woman is viewed as a sexually mature person. The setting in of the menses brings with it not only the ability and the right for full sexual life, but first and foremost the divine call to it, the unavoidable duty. The menstruating unmarried girl in a father's house is considered to be heavy sin and burden for him. Therefore, it is the aim of every father to marry off his daughter as soon as she achieves maturity.

"The girl must be married before the coming of menstruation." (Gautama XVII. 21: cited in Mayer 1971: 161)

If the father fails to marry his daughter by then, he is seen as guilty of *bhuan hatya*, the sin of embryo murder. The religious texts lay down that no menses should be wasted, for women is created in order that, she may in turn create. An unwed mature girl in a fathers' house thus is seen as source of great unhappiness and liability for the parents since it means that the father has failed to execute his religious duty. More important is the fact that "marriage is seen as the gateway to motherhood"[1] and motherhood is the greatest achievement in the life of a woman. Besides, for economic reasons too, desire to marry off their daughters as early as possible prevails, as this would reduce their burden of supporting the dependent unmarried daughters. Moreover, so much importance is given to a woman's "purity" that there is always the fear in the minds of parents that, if not married early, daughters' virginity might be violated. To avoid any kind of sexual harassment, parents condition their daughters to remain behind closed doors with limited or no interaction with other males. There are strict prescriptions about how the girl should dress, talk and even laugh to avoid attracting the attention of men. She is also told to avoid 'acting like a male' and always establish the feminine identity. "Considerable importance is attached to the way a girl carries herself, the way she sits, stands, talks and interacts with others. A girl should walk with soft-steps, so soft that they are barely audible to others. Taking long strides denotes masculinity. Girls are often rebuked for jumping, running, rushing to a place or hopping. These movements are considered parts of masculine behaviour, unbecoming of a female. However, the logic of the management of girl's sexuality also defines them as unfeminine, they can bring the contours of body into greater prominence and attract people's attention."[2]

In this chapter, thus, an attempt is made to examine some of these and other related issues on marriage, taking into consideration the young girls' as well as parents' perceptions in the context of the selected villages. The broad issues covered in this chapter include: age at marriage, perception of the adolescent girls on marriage and married life, attitude towards dowry, choice of spouse, girls' opinion on divorce and remarriage, role expectations from marriage, reasons of early marriage, experience of married life, consequences of marrying them young and above all, parents' viewpoint of marriage of daughters.

Age of Marriage

During the last four decades of independence, serious attempts have been made both by the GOI and NGOs' to propagate delayed marriage, for obvious reasons of controlling the population, as it would mean delayed childbirth. Besides, it is argued that delayed marriage would have a positive impact on the health of the women as also of the infants.

However, it appears that the age-old traditions die hard, this is evident from the data obtained from the selected villages. Out of 400 adolescent girls, as many as 87, i.e. 21.75 per cent were already married, and in 56 cases, i.e. 14.0 per cent marriage of the girls were already fixed and was to be solemnised shortly. In 37 cases, i.e. 9.25 per cent, negotiations were at the final stage.

In all such cases, parents were to marry their daughters in the then current year only. Thus, it is clear that in 45 per cent cases of the adolescent girls in the age group 10-16 years, marriage was either solemnised or fixed or under active negotiation. This amply speaks of our failure to convince a sizeable chunk of the population of the advantages of delayed marriage.

Table 5.1: Distribution of Adolescent Girls by Status of marriage

Married Status	No. of girls	Per cent
Married	87	21.75
Engaged	56	14.00
Active negotiation for marriage	37	9.25
Parents yet to decide	220	55.00
Total	**400**	**100.00**

Proximity to city life and exposure to media and modern living certainly delays the incidence of marriage. This is clear when we look at the incidence of marriage among young girls in three different sample regions. For example, in Delhi region in only 32.8 per cent of the adolescent girls, marriage was either solemnised or fixed or under active negotiation. In the villages of Bharatpur which were close to the city, but not so exposed to media and modern living as those in Delhi region, the incidence of marriage or those whose marriage were fixed or under active negotiation was relatively more at 35.6 per cent. Villages of Jaunpur which were completely in the interior and away from both media and modern living seem to stick to conventional norms of marrying daughters young. As many as 44.7 per cent of the adolescent girls in these village were married and in 20.4 per cent cases marriages were either fixed or under active negotiations. Details of the information can be seen from Table 5.2:

Table 5.2: Distribution of adolescent girls by status of marriage in their sample regions

	Delhi		Bharatpur		Jaunpur	
Marital Status	No.	percent	No.	percent	No.	percent
Married	10	14.3	18	9.1	59	44.7
Engaged	8	11.4	34	17.1	14	10.6
Active negotiation for marriage	5	7.2	19	9.6	13	9.8
Parents yet to decide	47	67.1	127	64.1	46	34.9
Total	**70**	**100.0**	**198**	**100.0**	**132**	**100.0**

On examining the age at marriage in three different regions, we get a disturbing picture. There were as many as 9 girls who got married at the age of 8-10 years only. In 28 cases, it was during the age of 11 to 12 years. There were 18 cases of girls marrying at 13 to 14 years. Adolescent girls marrying at 15-16 years numbered 32. Across three different regions, the picture varies widely. While in the case of villages in Delhi, there was none to marry before 12 years of age, in Bharatpur, there were only 9 cases to have married between 8-12 years. Jaunpur presented a more disturbing picture in the respect. Girls marrying even at the age of 8-10 years numbered as many as 7 out of 9 such observed cases in Jaunpur alone. In villages in close proximity to city life and open to media world, most of the young girls married at the age of 14-16 years. Table 5.3 throws sufficient light on this issue.

Table 5.3: Age at marriage of Adolescent girls in three regions

Age of marriage (years)	Total		Delhi		Bharatpur		Jaunpur	
	No.	%	No.	%	No.	%	No.	%
8-10	9	10.3	-	-	2	11.1	7	11.9
11-12	28	32.2	-	-	4	22.2	24	40.7
13-14	18	20.7	3	30.0	5	27.8	10	17.0
15-16	32	36.8	7	70.0	7	38.9	18	30.5
Total	**87**	**100.0**	**10**	**100.0**	**18**	**100.0**	**59**	**100.0**

Details can be seen from Table 5.4:

Table 5.4: Distribution of married girls by age of marriage and caste

Age at marriage (years)	Upper Caste		Intermediate Caste		Scheduled Caste	
	No.	percent	No.	percent	No.	percent
8-10	4	13.8	2	5.0	3	16.7
11-12	8	27.6	14	35.0	6	33.3
13-14	5	17.2	10	25.0	3	16.7
15-16	12	41.4	14	35.0	6	33.3
Total	**29**	**100.0**	**40**	**100.0**	**18**	**100.0**

Relating the age at marriage of the adolescent girls with parameters such as caste/religion, educational level of the girl and income levels of the parents, we observed that while among upper castes the incidence of marriage of young girls at early age was relatively higher than amongst the intermediate and scheduled castes. This was especially so in the interior villages.

However, education appeared to influence the age at marriage even in the interior villages. For example, while almost all the girls married before the age of 10 years were either illiterate or had education below primary level, those who married at the age of 15-16 years had mostly attended high school. This is evident from Table 5.5:

Table 5.5: Distribution of married young girls by levels of education and age at marriage

Age at marriage	Level of education			
	illiterate	primary	below high school	High school
8-10	7	2	-	-
11-12	12	7	9	-
13-14	4	8	6	-
15-16	9	8	13	2
Total	**32**	**25**	**28**	**2**

There seems to be no positive relationship between the age of marriage and the annual income levels of the parents. Parents with both low and high income levels appeared to be alike in marrying off their daughters at early age. This is clear from the data contained in Table 5.6.

Reasons for Early Marriage

On probing into the phenomenon of early marriage of growing young girls, we came across various reasons responsible for it. Interestingly, majority of the parents (290, i.e. 72.5 per cent) feared sexual insecurity, and therefore, prefered early marriage for their daughters. In 170 cases, i.e. 42.5 per cent, the parents preferred to marry off their girls at an early age because of religious prescriptions about marriage of girls before they attain puberty.

There were also reasons of shelving economic responsibility by marrying off girls as early as possible and passing on the responsibility of the girl to their in-laws. More important for parents was the reason of ensuring early social security for their daughters by marrying them early. This was more so in the cases of parents having more than two daughters. We came across parents having more than two daughters who were married off simultaneously to avoid double expenditure. In such cases, parents were obivious of the tender age of the younger girl.

Table 5.6: Distribution of married girls by age at marriage and income levels of the parents

Age at marriage	Income levels (Rs.)					
	Upto 5000		5000-10000		10000 and above	
	No.	%	No.	%	No.	%
8-10	2	6.9	3	8.8	4	16.7
11-12	10	34.5	13	38.2	5	20.8
13-14	7	24.1	6	17.6	5	20.8
15-16	9	31.12	12	35.3	10	41.7
Total	**29**	**100.0**	**34**	**100.0**	**24**	**100.0**

Surprisingly, a sizeable number of girls (192, i.e. 48.0 per cent) did not want to marry at such a young age. They generally preferred to marry at the age of 18-19 years. For 94 girls the ideal age of marriage was 20-21 years. But, there were also girls (101) who agreed to abide by the conventional form of early marriage between the age of 12 and 16 years. Those who were better educated (only 59) expressed their preference for marrying at the age of 22-25 years, only after completing their education.

• Paradoxically, a large number of girls do not themselves want to marry at an early age, but would accept it if decided so by their parents. In as many as 275 cases, the girls indicated that early marriage takes place due mainly to parents' wishes. Some girls were keen to marry at early age owing to the charms of new clothes and jewellery as also for the charm of new life that marriage promises. However, most of these girls were illiterate, were confined to the village atmosphere and were falling in the age group below 14 years. •

Table 5.7: Responses of parents and girls on reasons of early marriage

Reasons	No.	Per cent
(i) Parents viewpoint		
(a) Sexual insecurity	290	72.5
(b) Religious understanding	170	42.5
(c) Economic reasons	90	22.5
(d) Transfer of responsibility	125	31.25
(e) Ensuring early security	105	26.25
(ii) Girl's point of view		
(a) Did not want to marry early	192	48.0
(b) Fathers' wish	275	68.75
(c) Mothers' wish	-	-
(d) Charm for new clothes, etc.	45	11.25
(e) Charm for new life	50	14.00

Choice of Spouse

We also tried to explore the perception of the girls on the question of the choice of spouse. As one may expectin the Indian rural context, a vast majority (321) of the girls believed in the existing social practice of arranged marriage. It is a practice where parents and relatives of the girl through some middlemen look for the groom and settle the marriage. The marriage is usually settled and solemnised without taking the consent of the girls and boys. In most cases, the boys and the girls do not even see each other before marriage. Interestingly, among this lot, there were as many as 38 girls who expressed the desire to choose the spouse. Of these, 19 were educated upto middle and beyond but below high school. It may be stressed that out of those who believed in arranged marriages, 164 were from upper caste, 86 from intermediate caste and 67 from lower caste. This may indicate the rigidity with which the custom of arranged marriage is followed, especially among upper castes. It is also significant to note that, whereas, parents treat a girl who has acquired puberty as being an 'adult' and, therefore, consider them mature for marriage. However, such girls are not being allowed to participate in major decision-making processes, such as the age at marriage and choice of spouse. Education does not seem to have much influence on girl's response towards choice of spouse. The responses cut across both uneducated and the educated ones.

Parents were more vocal on the question of the choice of spouse. Excepting 26 and 8 cases of parents who gave no response or admitted ignorance, as many as 224 parents strongly felt that girls should not be left to choose their spouse. Most felt that it is the concern and responsibility of the parents to choose spouse for their daughters. There were only 93 parents who felt that the girls' opinion should also be taken into consideration. However, none of them was willing to allow their daughter to decide on their own to select the life partner. On asking as to why they feel that girls should not make a choice of their spouse, they generally believed that girls were not mature enough to take such decisions. They have no wordly experience. For many of them, the question itself appeared irrelevant and they preferred to ignore it.

Opinion on Divorce

Response on divorcc rcflected a strong family structure emphasizing particularly the central nature of the husband-wife relationship. Whereas, 196 girls felt that divorce was not a viable solution for domestic problems, 124 girls expressed that it was a solution. Most of the upper caste girls, i.e. 110, said it was not a solution and from the middle and lower castes this number was 4 and 40 respectively. Amongst the Muslims (7) 3 said that it was not a solution, whereas only 1 said that it was and three did not respond. Out of 196 girls, 80 were either uneducated or education was upto primary and 98 were middle and above.

In Delhi most of them favoured divorce. In Rajasthan majority was against divorce and in Jaunpur responses were divided equally.

On the question of the course of action they would resort to upon maltreatment by the husband, as many as 179 girls expressed the desire to resolve the differences or bear it, whereas, 92 girls would like to go back to their parents. The girls who wanted to return to their parents in such an eventuality were mostly in the age group of 14-16 years and from the upper caste. Of those who expressed the desire to resolve the matter amicably within the family or bear it, as many as 103 were educated. It clearly shows that girls who expressed the willingness to adjust were basically educated ones. It is contrary to the general belief that education leads to maladjustment in the family. These figures also indicate that with education, internalisation of norms related to family structure and the concept of ideal wife becomes stronger. For example, in group discussions girls mentioned about becoming an ideal wife like Sita. However, one should not miss the response given by 92 girls. All these girls categorically expressed that in such extreme eventuality they would seek legal help or leave the husband. If need be, they would take up some job so that they could feed and take care of their children. But, the option to leave the husband was seen as the last resort. Most of these girls came from intermediate and lower castes.

Contrary to the girls' response, a sizeable number of parents (281) strongly felt that in case of serious maladjustment, girls should resort to divorce. However, for 117 parents, divorce was no solution to marital disharmony. Those who would not give any response formed a negligible proportion.

On the Question of Dowry

The practice of demanding dowry is widely prevalent both in the interior villages as well as in the urban centres. It only differs in degree and form. Needless to say, it has assumed inhuman proportions, whereas, in instances of inadequate dowry, harassment and torture of the bride is common. In some cases, the in-laws and the husband do not hesitate to murder the bride. We also wanted to seek the opinion of the village girls on the question of dowry. Surprisingly, a large number of them (234) felt that dowry should be given, whereas only 18 girls strongly felt against the practice of dowry.On the contrary, most of the parents felt that dowry has assumed evil form and must stop without any delay. As many as 172 of them were giving dowry because it was a social practice. There were 89 parents who felt that if dowry is not given, the in-laws will ill-treat the girl. But, 36 of them had a different point to express. They felt that dowry would bring status and autonomy to their daughters.

On the question of giving a share in the parental property to the girl, again the parents were divided. There were 134 parents not willing to give any share in the family property to the girl. But they were willing to give dowry. In 174 cases, parents agreed to share the property equally among the children, including girls. Rest of the parents did not express any opinion on this. However, the majority of the girls preferred a share in the property to dowry. Since, the system of sharing family property did not exist, they were, therefore, not prepared to forego dowry.

Level of Consciousness of Married Girls on Issues like Child Birth, Child Care, Family Planning and Health Care

We observed a fairly large number of growing young girls marrying at an early age in our study area. One is then led to ask, are such girls prepared for leading a married life and are they aware of issues relating to childbirth and child care? In the contest of general debate and concern expressed regarding the high incidence of infant mortality due to ignorance on matters relating to child birth and child care, examination of those issues become all the more relevant for us. We decided to ascertain from the growing young girls their opinion on matters pertaining to pregnancy, motherhood, immunisation, special diet during pregnancy, cutting of the cord, cholestrum mother's milk feed, immunisation and child health care (diarrhoea). Questions were also asked about their level of understanding on family planning and their methods. We discuss below the responses of these girls on such issues.

Right at the outset it may be pointed out that many of these girls did not respond to such questions. They felt shy in answering them and mostly giggled. There is a social taboo on talking about such issues. In many a case, the parents got annoyed and prevented us from asking such questions. They did not think it proper to discuss such issues with young girls. Many of the parents (262) do not seem to acquaint the young girls about matters relating to childbirth, family planning, health care and other concerned issues. All that they imparted before marriage of the girl or at the time of 'Gauna' concerned to her responsibilities towards in-laws, husband and other members of the in-laws' family. However, there were quite a few (92) of the parents who thought girls can learn on such issues from other sources such as their friends and sisters-in-law. The rest of the parents abstained from responding.

Pregnancy

Regarding knowledge about pregnancy, almost all unmarried growing young girls simply evaded the question, as talking about sex is tabooed for them. However, the married ones did respond, though vaguely. For many of them (40 out of 87) pregnancy takes place only after marriage. There were only 26 of the married girls who knew that pregnancy can take place after the onset of menses. This clearly shows that knowledge of the young girls about pregnancy is almost absent. This however does not mean that they are not aware of sex life, since they are in close interaction with the natural environment of the village. This was evident from the way most of unmarried girls giggled on being asked this question in the group discussion.

Child Birth

When asked, if they knew anything about childbirth as many as 127 responded in the negative. All of them showed ignorance about this issue. But there were a few of them (52) who had knowledge about childbirth. A large majority (221) simply did not respond to this question.

Tetanus Innoculations

Tetanus innoculations to the pregnant mother to prevent infant mortality as also for saving the mother from danger to her life is medically a must. Measures on the same are increasingly taken by government agencies. However, it appears that quite a sizeable number of the married ones (87) and those engaged or likely to be married soon (9) did not know about it.

Nutritional Care During Pregnancy

Needless to say, birth weight of the child is directly related with the diet of the mother during pregnancy. One of the reasons of high infant mortality rate in India is considered to be due to low weight of the child at birth. This is caused mainly due to unbalanced and nutritionally poor food consumed by mother during pregnancy. We wanted to ascertain the knowledge of the young would-be-mother regarding the kind of food the pregnant mothers should take.

Surprisingly, all of the young future mothers appeared to know about the need of a balanced and nutiritious diet for pregnant mother. But often their ideas of what constitutes a nutritious and balanced diet was incorrect. For 86 out of 180 future mothers, ghee was a part of nutritional diet. Only 14 of them thought taking 'Dal' was desirable, whereas 42 emphasized green vegetables and, 55 considered milk as a balanced food. Only 5 of them considered non-vegetarian food as a need during pregnancy. Since non-vegetarian food is considered to be a hot food, girls are generally discouraged from consuming them, as it is thought to increase the sexual desires.

Cutting of the Umblical Cord

In rural India, another cause of high infant mortality is tetanus, through the use of a rusted old knife (chakku) for cutting the umbilical cord of the baby. This is the traditional practice widespread all over the countryside. To spread a new awareness against this practice, a massive campaign has been launched by UNICEF, WHO, GOI and NGOs. This was a good opportunity for us to assess how far the age old practice of using old knife for cutting the cord is being preferred to be replaced by sterilised knife or new blade. Interestingly, many of the married and those likely to be married in near future expressed that new blades should be used for cutting the cord, those who had nothing to say on this, or expressed their ignorance on this issue were mostly illiterate. This necessitates to continue spreading the message on the use of sterilised knife or new blade for cutting the cord.

Colostrum

The first milk of the mother is paradoxically treated as unhealthy and unclean for the child but with religious value. It is taken out after the childbirth and offered to the family god or simply thrown away. The most valuable element of colostrum in the first milk of the mother simply goes waste. Mothers are not aware of the importance of feeding the first milk to the newly born baby. Girls in our area of research do not seem to be an exception to this general practice, excepting those who were told of its importance through some women's development programme, implemented in Delhi and in parts of Bharatpur area. Girls in Jaunpur who are not exposed to any of such programme were almost unanimous in believing throwing away the first milk of the mother after offering the necessary 'Puja'.

Child Health Care

To understand the perception of the young girls on measures they preferred for child health care we asked a few test questions pertaining to breast feeding, immunisation and diarrhoea/rehydration therapy. Their responses are described below respectively:

a) Breastfeeding

Breastfeeding continues to be a widespread practice among the mothers. Even the young girls were unanimously in favour of breast feeding, with exceptions in the urban centres or under influence of modern living. Such girls, numbering only 26 out of 180 were married and shortly to be married. They were mostly from Delhi region. Nevertheless, girls differed on the duration of breast feeding. While 26 girls expressed that breast milk should be given for six months only, 53 girls advocated breast feeding upto 1 year. There were also girls (35) who advocated breast feeding upto 3 years. Those who felt that breast milk should be given till the birth of second child numbered 12 only. There were 54 girls who did not respond at all.

b) Immunisation

On the question of the sort of immunisations for the newly born baby, girls' responses varied widely. Except 36 cases, who did not know anything about immunisation, almost all of them had an idea about different type of immunisations. But, none of them knew fully about total immunisation package. While 11 girls knew about polio-drops, only 8 were aware of BCG and 62 had heard of tetanus injections. There were only 28 girls who knew about diphtheria vaccine, only 12 knew about cholera injection and 76 about measles. There is, thus, a strong need to familiarise and encourage practice of the total package of immunisation programmes.

c) Treating the Diarrhoea Cases

Deaths due to diarrhoea, especially among the infants is very common in the rural areas. This is caused by dehydration. The moment a child suffers from loose motions, the family members usually stop giving them any water. This is feared to aggravate the problem. On the contrary, medically it is advised to give more water with a mix of salt, sugar and lemon in such a situation. In our universe, 148 out of 180 married and likely to be married girls knew about giving water to the child suffering from loose motions and vomiting. But, 30 such girls did not agree with the idea of giving water to the child in such a situation. However, very few girls (25) knew about oral rehydration therapy, which is in common understanding, a mix of salt, sugar and lemon given with water.

Family Planning

It was quite interesting to discuss the issues regarding family planning and method of birth control with married girls. As it was a sensitive subject, mostly treated as tabooed, it became difficult to extract their views on this issue. However with extra efforts by making private conversations with married girls with the help of the investigators from the village, we could gather some information on the question of family planning and birth control.

On talking to 180 married and shortly to be married girls, it was observed that as many as 100 of them preferred a small family, whereas, 40 had no desire for family planning. Forty of them did not respond to the questions.

Only 21 of these girls knew about the method of birth control. But none of them responded as to whether they practice any form of birth control measures or not. They were aware of only two forms of birth control measures, 17 of them knew about operations and only 4 about contraceptives. Regarding the source of knowledge about such birth control measures, 14 of them came to know through sister-in-law or mother-in-law, 3 of them knew through hospitals and 4 from the media. This calls for a serious attempt to propagate the use of all forms of media and information channels to educate the population at large, especially the young girls, about the importance of family planning and methods available for birth control. Addressing such exercise to young girls will be more meaningful, rather than covering the older women who already have many children. It is all the more important to address family planning issues in the context of the health of the young girls rather than only emphasising on birth control.

Conclusion

It is amply clear from the discussions in the foregoing sections that these young girls are not prepared, mentally as well as physically, for marriage. They lack sufficient/adequate information about marriage and motherhood. They are also not aware of the new roles expected of them after marriage. All this has various consequences for young girls. They have to create a separate space for themselves, in the family, unknown to them. Besides, they are not prepared for a marital role, neither aware of family planning methods and child care. Socialisation process inculcates values of tolerance and self restraint. Secondly, they accept any kind of treatment meted out to them in the house of their in-laws. They might be harassed and tortured, but would not complain. Since they are raised to practice denial, they are the last ones to eat in the family of in-laws. This has an adverse effect on the growing reproductive system of their bodies. As new brides, they can not complain about themselves even if they have serious health problems. Marriage at early age also leads to early childbirth. As their reproductive systems are not mature enough, early childbirth creates health hazards for the mother as well as the infants. It has also been established by other studies that delayed marriage will have effect on declining fertility rate. Due to their ignorance of birth control practices, these young girls are caught in the cycle of child production, which often leads to negative consequences for their health.

Chapter Six

Health Situation of Young Girls in Rural Areas

In trying to understand the problems and needs of adolescent girls in rural areas, the issues related to their health-situation need consideration. The village environment interacts with human biology in the context of the socio-cultural reality of the young girls in the rural setting. In this section, we touch upon *a)* the reality of the menstruating girl, *b)* discrimination against the young girls in terms of access to food, *c)* her place in the eating pattern, *d)* hygienic conditions at the personal and village level and *e)* information and knowledge about health and hygiene along with its sources.

In the villages selected for study, the average age at menstruation of young girls is fourteen years; and is to some extent conditioned by societal influences such as the menarcheal difference between upper and lower classes among Hindus, and the inter-generational menarcheal age differences, as cited by Sebald.[1] Other factors like the phenomenon of scarcity and deprivation affecting the menstrual age, especially among the agrarian population, are related to the delayed emotional development compared to the urban situation. This is especially so, since modern scientific standards concerning nutrition, sanitation, hygiene and medication, and dissemination of knowledge are more prevalent in urban areas than in the rural areas.

These girls, as we have seen, are socialized to play expressive roles, i.e. social roles within the private domain of the family, unlike their brothers who are trained to play the instrumental roles, i.e. to take up the responsibility of productive functions in the public domain.[2] May be this role expectation leads to discrimination vis-a-vis the 'productive members' of the family. The subjects in our study are victimized in terms of the nutritional support that they get from their family even though they may be working more than their brothers, both within and outside the household. For instance, milk was offered to the sons mainly to make them stronger so that they could enter the public domain confidently. Whereas, girls, who are the potential mothers, were not allowed to pay attention to their physical development. If a girl ate at her will she was seen to be 'grazing', a colloquial usage to describe usurpation of food.

Moreover, there is restriction regarding the kind of food they can eat. Thus, a menstruating girl, as observed by Leela Dube, is asked not to eat spicy food, pickles and curds, and in general to avoid what are considered very 'cold' or very 'hot' foods.[3]

Table 6.1: Eating Pattern in the Villages

	Eating Pattern	No. of families
1.	Old members eat first	58
2.	Father eats first	188
3.	Mother eats first	1
4.	children eats first	103
5.	All eat together	5
6.	Men eat first followed by women and children together	2
7.	Men and children eat first followed by the women	43
	Total	**400**

Girls are discriminated against even in terms of when they are allowed to take their meals. In 58 families, old members of the house were offered the meal first; in 188 families the father was served the food before anyone else; in only 1 family did the mother eat before others; in 103 families children were served meals before anyone else, but we observed that in almost all cases it was male children and not female. In fact, in no family did the girls eat first and in 43 families men and children ate together after which the women ate by themselves. It is most striking to note that none among the girls mentioned a case where there is no fixed order of eating, which indicates the rigid systems of practices operating in these villages.

Table 6.2: Discrimination in Diet of Boys and Girls

	Diet Pattern	Percentage of number of families
1.	No response	10.5
2.	Girls and Boys should be given the same diet	57.5
3.	Ignorance of the diet requirement	12.25
4.	Diet of boys and girls should not be the same	3.5
5.	Allow sons and daughters to eat as much as they require	3.0
6.	Girls generally eat less	13.25
	Total	**100.00**

In contrast to actual practice 57.5 per cent of the parents agreed that girls and boys should be given the same kind of diet in quantity and quality. 10.5 per cent of the parents did not respond to this question whereas, 12.25 per cent of the parents professed ignorance on this matter. Only 3.5 per cent of the parents felt that the diet of the sons should be better in quality and quantity than of the daughters be the same. Only 3 per cent of the parents allowed their sons and daughters to eat as much as they would want to. 13.25 per cent of the parents somehow felt that generally the girls eat less compared to boys. Moreover, even though 57.5 per cent agreed in principle, in practice none made a conscious attempt to provide adequate nourishment to their daughters.

This sex bias in nutrition for the sons and against the daughters is clearly exposed. These young girls enter into marriage and motherhood in an undernourished state.

The cultural pattern of women being the last ones to eat and often eating least both quantitatively and qualitatively has further negative effects on their health situation. Thus, these young girls manage to get only a poor share of the nutritional resources available to the family.

The problem of poor sanitation and lack of access to safe drinking water also has been an adverse effect on the health of these young girls. In many of our villages, sanitation is extremely poor. In most of the villages an open drainage system was functional. Not having access to safe drinking water created health and hygiene complications. Further, even where vegetable and fruits were available, there was ignorance about health and nutritional education.

Discrimination is more marked in case of expensive food items like milk, eggs, fruits etc. observes VHAI. Moreover susceptibility to respiratory diseases due to poor ventilation and inhalation of pollutants is very high for these girls.

Dr. Gopalan, in his study on Nutrition and Nation Building argues that the non-formal channel for educating girls between 10-17 years old make the differences to the upbringing (health, nutrition and education) of the coming generation. Their vocational training should include hygiene, nutrition, farm technology, sex education, family planning, child-care and home nursing.[4]

Information regarding health issues in the rural areas is rather poor. In our case, even though half or majority of the girls in some villages had some information about various health related matters, their knowledge was cursory and inadequate even on those matters which they know. Many of them were aware of the various diseases endemic in their localities along with their remedies. Because of the immunization scheme, knowledge of BCG, DPT, Polio and Tetanus infections was on the finger tips of many girls, specially in villages near the urban areas. Yet, regarding menstruation young girls knew very little when questions related to it were raised in the group discussions. Generally speaking, it was either their mother or friends who imparted knowledge about menstruation to them. Only 46.75 percent of girls were informed about it by their mothers and 13.25 percent by their friends.

Table 6.3: On the Question of Personal Hygiene

Practices	Percentage of No. of girls
1. Use clean cloth	46.50
2. Use any cloth or rags	24.25
3. Use cotton wool	8.00
4. Use sanitary napkins	1.50
5. No response	2.25
6. Not menstruating	17.50
Total	**100.00**

An unhygienic practice was found amongst the menstruating girls as is obvious from the above table. 24.25 percent of the girls used any cloth or rags during menses, whereas, only 8 percent of the girls used cotton wool. Only 1.5 percent used sanitary napkins and most of these girls belonged to the villages surrounding Delhi. Even though they seemed to have knowledge about it, yet they washed their hair only once in ten days or even just once a month; not surprisingly, many had lice in their hair. Girls also mentioned about the importance of keeping their nails, teeth, body and clothes clean along with not exposing food to flies and mosquitoes. However, during the group discussions in most of the villages, specially those of Jaunpur, girls wore tidy dresses but none of them had clean hands, and properly cleansed and manicured nails.

Regarding the knowledge about sex determination, most of the girls believed that God determines it, although, eventually the woman gets blamed for not producing a son. In fact, the educated girls in Rangpuri, a village near Delhi, felt particularly shy about discussing such matters. They were too shy and inhibited to even lift their heads and face the interviewers. The uneducated girls in some villages of Bharatpur and the educated girls of Jaunpur villages were quite vocal about it and the girls of Jaunpur villages in particular blamed the woman for not giving birth to a son.

In the village Malahe of the Bharatpur district information on health and hygiene was very poor. It should be noted here that no school exists for girls in Malahe. However, in Noh, Nogayan and Peepla, only a few girls were familiar with health related issues. In Jaunpur villages, on the contrary, most of the girls were well aware of their health situation and, in fact, spoke critically about the lack of health facilities for the villagers.

It is significant to note here that even if there are health services available in the villages in terms of primary health-centre or a doctor vaid, many girls do not visit them when ill. For instance, in Sewar, Kamlesh has been married for the last eight years and is still childless. However, she has never visited a doctor and feels as if she is living a degraded and shamed life.

Sources of Information on Bodily Changes

Girls in most of the villages lack scientific knowledge about the physical and harmonal changes in their bodies. It comes to them as an underhand information mostly from their friends. The mothers, at times, impart information about menstruation to their daughters. However, with their mothers or aunts they feel too reluctant and shy to discuss such matters related to childbirth, menstruation, etc. Proximity to the animal world and Nature becomes another source of information, besides the television, radio and magazines. Thus, it becomes imperative to introduce sex and health related education for these young girls in the rural areas.

Chapter Seven

Status of Education and Her Awareness

In this section we shall analyse the level of education and general awareness of these girls. What are the educational opportunities available to these girls? To what extent do they avail of them and how many? What are the various structural and social constraints which, if they do, prevent the maximal utilisation of such facilities? How do these girls relate education to their everyday reality - do they perceive any benefits of education? These are some of the questions out of the myriad our study addressed itself to regarding these young girls.

The sample of 400 is heterogenous - we have both educated and uneducated girls. The category of educated includes girls who had been to school at some point of time but have dropped out. Table 7.1 gives their educational profile:

Table 7.1: Educational Profile of Sample girls

Level of education	No. of girls	Per cent
No response	63	15.75
Uneducated	72	18.00
Upto primary	85	21.25
Upto middle	75	18.75
Upto secondary	75	18.75
Upto Higher Secondary	30	7.50
Total	**400**	**100.00**

Out of the sample of 400 girls 15.75 per cent girls didn't respond to the question about their educational status, 18 per cent were uneducated and 21.25 per cent were educated upto primary, 18.75 upto middle; 18.75 upto secondary and 7.5 upto higher secondary. Thus, whereas 21.25 per cent girls are at primary levels only 7.5 per cent or nearly one third continue upto the Higher Secondary level. There is a sudden decline in numbers after reaching the secondary level, whereafter from 18.75 per cent, the number decreases to a mere 7.5 per cent.

As for the total percentage of dropouts at various levels, out of the total 66.25 per cent who have been to the school, 18.25 per cent have dropped out at various levels, the highest being at the secondary level.

A majority (56.25) of the school going girls in our sample joined school at the age of five years (see Table 4.5, Chapter IV). However, some (24.47) didn't know the age and, therefore, didn't respond. A very small percentage of 3.12 and 1.04 joined at the age of 6 and 7 years respectively. In our sample, thus, the otherwise widespread phenomenon of sending girls to school late doesn't hold true. However, dropping out a year or two after reaching puberty (average age in our sample is 14 years) does hold true for the majority.

Maximum of 36.45 per cent school going girls are in class IV, followed by 22.91 in class VIII and 19.27 per cent in class X. The table below may indicate the levels at which girls drop out - if they join school, they continue till primary (class IV or V) if they get a chance beyond that, they go upto class VIII and in the third stage till class X. There is a sharp decrease in the number of girls at levels immediately after each of these (i.e. sixth, ninth and eleventh).

What are the reasons for such a trend? Why do girls if they do at all join school, drop out at certain levels? Many structural constraints coupled with the socio-economic reality, and traditional attitudes and opinion, hinder their access to the almost marginal and in some cases non-existent educational facilities for the girls. More important is the belief of both the girl and her parents that the existing formal education is of no use. It has no bearing on her immediate reality and the girl fails to identify it with her future prospects. Yet quite a few girls expressed a strong desire to learn.

Table 7.2: Class-wise Distribution of School-going girls

Class	No. of girls	Per cent
No response	5	2.60
First	3	1.60
Second	4	2.08
Third	-	-
Fourth	70	36.45
Fifth	8	4.16
Sixth	10	5.20
Seventh	-	-
Eighth	44	22.91
Ninth	11	5.73
Tenth	37	19.27
Eleventh	-	-
Total	**192**	**100.00**

For the purposes of clarity we shall look at the structural and social constraints separately. However, it must be made clear that the two are not independent and instead continuously act upon and determine one another. Thus, whereas in some cases absence of a certain infrastructural facility, like a girl's school may prevent a girl from getting educated, in other cases, despite the presence of a school, parents' negative attitude towards daughter's education may be the reason for her not being educated. The two factors act in conjunction in a situation where the absence of one ratifies the presence of other, viz. absence of a girl's school ratifies parents attitude of not sending her to school.

To the question why they do not go to school, we got the following responses:

Table 7.3: Reasons for not going to School

Response	10-12	12-14	14-16	Total	Per cent
No response	31	37	124	192	48.0
No girls' school	2	6	7	15	3.75
School at distance	0	5	13	18	4.50
Parents don't send	5	15	30	50	12.5
Household work prevents	1	10	32	43	10.75

Don't feel like going	2	1	17	20	5.00
No particular reason	5	6	17	28	7.00
Getting married	1	0	12	13	3.25
Financial problem	1	4	15	20	6.00
Is a grown-up girl	0	0	1	1	0.25
Total				**400**	**100.00**

Structural Constraints: Education and Rural Development

"The map of illiteracy coincides almost exactly with the map of poverty".[1] The backwardness of the rural areas, the non-availability and in some cases the absence of basic educational facilities to a large extent determine the educational status of the villagers. In a situation of general scarcity and poverty, the girl in the rural areas is doubly disadvantaged because of her sex and her environment.

The availability or non-availability of educational facilities and opportunities and their relationship with the girl's reality takes various forms. For instance, why a girl doesn't go to school could be due to:

(a) there is no school in the village;
(b) there is a school, but it is at a distance or is in the nearby village;
(c) there is a school in the village but it is co-educational

No School in the Village

Except for two villages in Jaunpur (Heerapur and Baghela) all the other villages of our study have at least a primary school. However, the school being at a distance and the total absence of an exclusive girls' school* in the village were given as reasons for not attending school; e.g. in Malahe and Noh at Bharatpur the absence of a girls' school prevents girls from being educated. Thus, whereas 18 girls (4.5 per cent) said that the school was at a distance, 15 (3.74 per cent) said that they don't attend school because it is a co-educational one.

School at Distance

It is interesting to see that out of these 33 girls, 20 are from the age group 14-16 years as compared to 11 from the age group 12-14 years, 2 from 10-12 years. These numbers may seem small but when seen in the context of the parents' worry and anxiety about their grown up girls' safety, they seem quite large. A post-pubertal girl, is seen as a security risk. Due to the absence of a girls' school in the village, parents do not send their daughters to school because of the fear of misbehaviour or molestation or getting raped on the way. In Peepla, at Bharatpur, girls complained of living in an uncongenial 'mohalla' (colony) that prevented them from attending school. In fact, Poonam wants to study but is going to be married off as the Mohalla is not 'OK'.*

No School for Girls only

A similar argument is given regarding co-educational schools. Although parents let their daughters attend co-educational school upto primary level, beyond that they withdraw their daughters. The fear of their daughters getting 'spoilt' in the company of boys and consequently their reputations being tarnished is quite overpowering. The rule is not applied very strictly in the case of pre-pubertal girls. In our sample, only two girls from the age group 10-12 years said that absence of a girls' school prevented them from getting education. None of the girls from this age group talked about school being at a distance.

Ill-equipped and Maladministered Schools

For the girls who are going to the school, the problem of infrastructural constraints acquires a different dimension. They face the problem of ill-equipped and maladministered schools.

Table 7.4: Problems at School

Response	No. of girls	Per cent
No response (includes uneducated and the drop outs)	208	52.0
Drinking water	35	8.75
Electricity	3	.75
Teachers don't teach	8	2.00
Lack of equipments	11	2.75
Cleanliness	3	.75
No library	0	-
No games	1	.25
No means of transport	9	2.25
No problems	122	30.05
Total	**400**	**100.00**

The 'no response' in the above table are the girls who are not going to the school or have dropped out. Out of the 192 school going girls 70 (36.46 per cent) were able to identify some or the other problem, the remaining 122 (63.54 per cent) were unable to do so. Out of the 70, 35 girls complained of lack of drinking water facilities. It is interesting to see that most of these girls are from Delhi. They also mentioned lack of transport facilities as the schools are at a distance. Quite ironically, the girls from areas of Rajasthan where availability of potable water is an acute problem, failed to pinpoint the same.

Teachers' Indifference and Carelessness

However, some of them did talk about teachers' indifference and carelessness in the class. In fact, at Jaunpur, a girl complained of repeated beatings by the school teacher and hence, expressed the unwillingness to join school again. The girls also complained of lack of equipments and study-aids in school. Our village profile and a survey of the existing facilities project a grim picture. The school buildings are in a dilapidated state. Although some kind of training is given to girls, it is restricted to knitting, stitching, embroidery and cooking. Only some girls informed us about handicrafts and games. The others, i.e. 63.54 per cent girls were unable to identify any problems. They were resigned to a situation of denial and deprivation and didn't question it. The reinforcement of traditional norms and values by teachers in schools makes the situation even more difficult, therefore, there is a need to reorient structures in which these girls are put. Existing schools in rural areas do not provide an alternative. But is it just the absence of adequate facilities which prevent a girl from getting the required information and knowledge? No. "The most important single factor affecting girls' and women's progress is the prevailing attitude to education in the area where they live. If classes are conducted in the face of disapproval in addition to material difficulties, perseverance in studying can become an ordeal that few women can face. Hence the high rate of drop outs."[2]

Socio-economic Constraints: Negative Attitudes Towards Education

"Pad-likh kar kya karegi? Shadi ke bad tou chulha hi jhonkna hai - kya faida?" (What will she do by studying? After marriage she will just be confined to the kitchen. So what is the benefit ?). This is the answer one would generally get on asking the girls' parents about her education. Do parents actually feel this, or, do they once in a while when pressed to the corner think differently ? It is not that parents fail to see the benefit of education for their daughter. They do, but in a limited manner.

In our sample 50 girls (12.5 per cent) said that their parents do not send them to school. However, the other reasons like 'household work prevents'; 'no particular reason'; 'getting married'; 'is a grown up girl', etc. are also manifestations of a negative attitude towards the girls' education. What are the reasons for such an attitude?

There is no Money to Educate Girls

The reasons are both economic and social. Many parents do not send their daughters because they can't afford to. In our sample 5 per cent girls affirmed this.

Expenditure on girls education is economic loss for the Family

Majority of the parents consider expenditure on girls' schooling as an economic loss because in spite of spending on her dress, books, fees, etc., the parents will not get anything in return. Moreover, because a daughter is to be married off, it is wise to save money for her dowry rather than educate her, for a handsome dowry would fetch her a good husband but education may not.

Thus, in our study, on being asked if daughters should be educated as are sons, 69.46 per cent parents said that only sons should be educated. Why this should be so, majority (83.38 per cent) choose not to respond. However, the ones who responded did say that daughters will get married and leave. It is, therefore, 'advisable' to save for her dowry rather than spend on her education.

Parents' Fear of Getting Daughter's Virginity Violated

On the other hand, parents who can afford to send their daughters to school do not do so because of social customs and practices. Their major concern being the daughters' marriage, her reputation is precious. In our sample 3.25 per cent girls said that since they are going to be married soon, they had to discontinue schooling. In Noganya at Bharatpur, a girl failed in class X at the Peepla high school and is married. Though she has filled up the forms, she is not sure if she'll appear for the examinations. The parents fear that 'people may talk' about their daughters - she'll be seen as 'modern' and thereby of 'loose character'. Since she is the *izzat* of the family, she must be protected. Their responsibility ends with her marriage. In fact literally, lock, stock and barrel, she is transferred to another man and his family. She then becomes a *bahu - dusare khandan ki izzat*[*] - and numerous restrictions on her include the termination of her education. Society, thus, takes pride-in-women and acquiring respect and status through its control over women rather than giving respect to women.

Education might make the daughter "argumentative"

In fact, parents do not send their daughter to school, also because they see formal school education as having a negative effect on their daughter. The fear of her becoming 'argumentative' - *jyada munh chalayegi*[**] and the consequent problems she would get into at her *sasural*[***] acts as a restraint. Parents would much rather prefer her to be submissive, and hence, the entire gamut of do's and don'ts that entail her 'social programming' wherein education is merely a 'stop-gap' arrangement till the time she gets married.

Relevance of education of girls is seen as ability to write letters

This however, does not mean that education is 'useless'. When pressed to the limit, most of the parents did agree that if they were educated they would have been better off. In fact they did point out its manifold benefits. Thus, parents felt that if their daughter is educated she can stand on her own feet and support herself in times of adversity. Only if she is educated can she educate her children. In our study 40.89 per cent parents saw letter writing as a benefit of education. Some (15.65 per cent) even said that the girl can become a teacher. However when asked about educating our respondents majority of the parents (47.20 per cent) said it is of no use.

It is noteworthy that not only the parents who were themselves educated wanted to educate their daughters, but in fact, their daughters expressed strong desire to be educated. In Peepla (Bharatpur) for instance, Neelam wants to become a professor like her father who teaches English. In Jaunpur, Dulari wants to go and see places like her educated brother working in Bombay can do.

The invisible work-load

Another significant reason which prevents a girl from attending school is household work, particularly where the girl is the eldest in the sibling hierarchy. Nearly eleven per cent of the girls (43) in our sample stated that household work prevents them from attending school. Whereas, 28 (7 per cent) did not wish to express any reason, out of the 50 (12.5 per cent) who said their parents do not send them to school majority were observed to be engaged in helping in household chores or were too "grown up" (by local standards) to be sent to school. Thus, if these two categories are also added, the number of girls not going to school due to household work increases considerably.

Out of the 43 who clearly stated household work, the majority are from the lower castes and educated upto only primary level.

That most of these girls are from the lower caste may indicate the possibility of their working as maid servants and hence not being able to attend school.

Table 7.5: Castewise Break-up

Caste	No. of girls	Per cent
No Response	--	--
Hindu Upper Caste	8	18.60
Hindu Middle Caste	14	32.55
Hindu Lower Caste	19	44.20
Muslim	2	4.65
Total	**43**	**100.00**

Table 7.6: Educational Level

Level of Education	No. of girls	Per cent
No Response	7	16.28
Uneducated	9	20.93
Upto Primary	19	44.20
Upto Middle	4	9.30
Upto Secondary	1	2.32
Upto Higher Secondary	3	6.97
Total	**43**	**100.00**

Going by the fact that 44.20 per cent of these girls were educated up to primary and keeping in mind that majority of them, i.e. 74.41 per cent are from the age group 14-16 years, it may be concluded quite safely that once the daughters reach the primary level, they drop out of school and stay at home to do the household work. It demonstrates the widespread attitude of 'just' primary education being essential for the girl so that she can read and write. After that she must learn the household tasks and stay at home waiting to get married. The girl performs a variety of tasks varying from cleaning the house, washing clothes, cooking food to looking after her siblings. She goes out at the farm as well. All this is irrespective of whether she is school going or non-school going.

Thus Zareena, at Rangpuri in Delhi, left school because her parents forced her to do so owing to the amount of work to be done at home. In fact, during the group discussions, Mobina, who has passed Class VII and is already married came in late as she was busy working at home. Similarly, at Malipura and Sewar in Bharatpur many girls wished to go to school but said their parents do not allow as they have to work at home and take care of the cattle. There are similar examples at Jaunpur. Moreover, in case the younger sister was school-going, she had to stay back at home once her elder sister got married, and contribute to household chores.

Benefits of Education: Perception of the Young Girls

The girls who are able to attend school despite these numerous odds share their opinion regarding benefits of education with those not going to school. A good many girls contended that education (formal) has no bearing on their immediate reality. The benefits of education were seen mostly in terms of letter writing.

Table 7.7: Distribution of Responses on Education

Responses	Age Groups				
	10-12	12-14	14-16	Total	Per cent
No Response	22	29	59	110	27.5
It is useless	3	7	26	36	9.0
Letter-writing	8	17	61	86	21.5
Employment	7	19	38	64	16.0
Economic Independence	2	5	18	25	6.25
Personality Development	4	4	43	51	12.75
Awareness increases	1	4	23	28	7.00
	47	**85**	**268**	**400**	**100.00**

21.5 per cent girls saw the ability to write letters as the only benefit of education. 16 per cent were able to relate it to the possibility of being employed, only 6.25 per cent girls perceived economic independence as a consequence of employment. While 12.75 per cent girls said that education leads to personality development, 7 per cent said it results in an increase in awareness. A significant 9 per cent thought education as being of no use and 27.5 per cent girls did not respond to this question.

The majority of 110, i.e. 27.5 per cent girls did not respond, indicates that there is a lack of understanding about the benefits of education. Most of these girls (59) are from the age group 14-16 years.

Table 7.8: Level of Education

Response	Uneducated	Upto Prim.	Upto Midd.	Upto Sec.	Upto Higher Sec.	Total
No Response	12	22	33	26	17	110
It is useless	20	6	2	7	1	36
Letter-writing	32	30	16	5	3	86
Employment	17	25	15	4	3	64
Economic Independence	10	3	5	5	2	25
Personality Development	13	7	4	26	1	51
Awareness raising	6	9	3	9	1	28

Out of those who didn't respond, most girls (68) are from the upper caste and 68 are educated beyond the primary level. Thus, 61.81 per cent girls despite being educated fail to see the benefits of education. However, out of those who said it is useless, most of the girls are uneducated (16 out of 36). Moreover out of the 85 who cited the ability to write letter as the chief benefit, most girls are from lower caste (37) and are either uneducated (22) or only upto primary level (24).

The above statistics indicate that in the village situation, early marriage being the norm, the girls perceived the benefit of education only in terms of informing their parents about their well being and in situations of adversity faced in the in-laws' family. In our sample, this is more so in the case of lower caste and uneducated girls who treat education as synonymous with literacy. In fact, majority of parents (40.89 per cent) also see benefits of education in terms of letter writing only.

Employment

It is significant to see that 64 girls are able to relate education to employment. Most of them are from upper and middle castes and are educated at least upto primary and above levels. However, only 6.25 per cent are able to relate it with economic independence.

Some girls expressed the usefulness of education in terms of an increase in their awareness level and personality development. It is noteworthy that most of them are educated and, hence, it can be safely concluded that education does help in the identification of its benefits, i.e. girls who are not educated mostly see it as useless or only in terms of letter writing, but those who are educated are able to identify other benefits also.

The understanding of the benefits of education varies in different areas. In our sample, girls from the villages of Delhi talked of employment, whereas girls in Bharatpur said letter-writing and in Jaunpur personality development.

Table 7.9: Distribution of respondents on the benefits of education

Sample size	Area	Maximum response	No.	Per cent
70	Delhi	Employment	19	41.42
198	Bharatpur	Letter-writing	71	35.85
132	Jaunpur	Personality Development	37	28.03

Situating these villages on a continuum of the semi-urban (Delhi), those near to the city (Bharatpur) and the very interior (Jaunpur), we find that the infrastructural development of the village and its proximity to the urban centre plays a significant role in determining the attitudes towards education and its benefits. For instance in Delhi villages, where the girls are relatively more exposed to the urban culture, they have more information, more opportunities and more choices. They associate education with gainful employment. Kavita wants to become a policewoman but, more importantly, she wants to be educated and economically independent. If she can't become a police-woman, she'll become a nurse because her uncle works in Giridharilal Hospital as an electrician. Therefore, it will be easy for her to have access and information about the courses in nursing. In Bharatpur, on the other hand, girls talked about letter-writing. Most of these girls (44) are either uneducated or educated only upto primary. In Jaunpur villages despite their backwardness, the maximum response, being personality development ("*Sakshiyat Ubharti hai*") is owing to the fact that a centre is being run in the nearby village where various Chetna Nirman Camps, Legal Literacy Camps, etc., have been organised quite frequently. The girls here, therefore, identified benefits of education with personality development.

The perception of the benefits of education thus varies. Yet, by and large the girls are unable to relate it to their immediate reality. Is the situation then actually so grim or is there a ray of hope? Paradoxically, though the girls perceive benefits of education in a limited manner, almost all of them when asked expressed a strong desire to study. Even those who said otherwise, did not say so because they did not want to study but because they couldn't (e.g., some thought they were grown up enough as in Sewar) or that it was too late). Whereas 29 per cent didn't respond when asked if they would like to study or continue studying, 49.5 per cent said 'yes', 20.25 per cent said they would not like to study.

On being asked about the level upto which they would like to study they said Class VIII and X. Thus 64.14 per cent girls said Class VIII and X, only 25 girls said Class XII and just 8 said B.A. This shows that the girls are brought up and conditioned to internalize and subsequently reflect the existing norms regarding the 'required/adequate level of education' for a girl as being just Class VIII or X. This coincides with her age at menstruation as well.

Information and her level of awareness

The level of awareness is not an absolute category. In our study, situating this girl at the centre, the indicators used to assess her awareness relate to issues regarding health and hygiene; marriage, legal rights, science and technology and information about her immediate surroundings, i.e. her village in networking with the rest of the system.

The study attempts not merely to analyse the differences in levels of awareness in terms of disparate sources and channels through which information on selected issues is disseminated to the girl, it also endeavours to explain why, in situations, where despite the availability of and access to information, it is not utilized. Thus, a distinction between 'mere information' and its 'application' (awareness) is made.

In our sample, we observed that girls from semi-urban villages, who are school going and have access to sources of information like television, newspapers, books, magazines, etc., are better informed than the ones from interior villages and non-school going girls. In the case of girls from very backward regions (e.g. villages of

Jaunpur). A family member (usually brother or husband) working in the city is a valuable source of information. Where there is access to media, and other sources of information, it was found, as in the two villages of Delhi under study and to some extent in the villages of Bharatpur under study, that these girls, especially the educated ones, make use of them to gain information, and have, in fact, a considerable level of awareness on social issues, current national problems, geographical knowledge, importance and benefits of education, etc.

This holds true for other issues as well. In both the villages of Delhi and some at Bharatpur, girls were quite well informed about different kinds of vaccination like BCG, DPT, Polio, and Tetanus. However, very few knew about complicated issues like what determines the sex of the child. Majority believed that God determines it although the woman usually gets blamed for it when she has a daughter. (For information and awareness on health related issues please see the respective sections on health and marriage).

On issues regarding Science and Technology, girls were asked questions on solar cooker, smokeless chulha and their benefits. In the context of the village and keeping in mind that most of the time the girls are confined to the kitchen, knowledge of the above two may indicate their level of information. Whereas 44.75 per cent girls (179) haven't heard about either solar cooker or smokeless chulha, 3.75 per cent (15) have heard about it but not seen it while 38.5 per cent (154) girls have seen but never used it. Only 13 per cent (52) girls said that it is used in their houses. Most of the girls however, were able to indicate their benefits in terms of 'saves energy and effort', 'does not blacken the wall', 'does not harm the eyes because no smoke', etc.

On matters regarding their village, girls were quite well informed. The duties of the Gram Pradhan was seen as primarily being an arbitrator, of maintaining cleanliness in the village and making roads. Girls were able to identify the benefits of the post office in terms of sending letters, money orders and even opening savings accounts. They were able to tell us if a programme for women was being run in the village.

The girls, therefore are informed but the available information and facility even where present, is not utilized. The presence of a TV in the villages shouldn't be treated as an adequate source of information because not all girls have access to it. Moreover, those who have are allowed to watch only some programmes. Rajni, at Kishangarh in Delhi, is not allowed to watch TV at all as her parents feel that she'll get spoilt and would elope with someone!

Similarly even if there is a centre in the village, parents do not let their daughters go because of the fear of misbehaviour on the way. The restrictions on the girl's mobility, thus, hinder her exposure and possibility of acquiring information. In fact, the school going girls are on a relatively better footing due to their mobility - even though a restricted one.

Conclusively, thus, limited sources of information coupled with the socialization process determine the girl's level of information and awareness. Even if she has information, she doesn't utilise it as she doesn't value it. Or she doesn't have an access and opportunity to utilise the information she has acquired through limited sources.

Chapter Eight

*Imperceptible Transference of Work-Roles**

This section looks at young girls in rural India through the perspective of their diverse domestic and non-domestic tasks and aims to determine how these work roles literally leave no space and time for the phenomenon of adolescence to occur. At what cost do these young girls play these work-roles prematurely shall also be our concern here.

These young girls, as we have maintained cannot be viewed as a homogeneous group. Differences arising from variation in region, caste, community, education and the rural-urban environment, tend to make these young girls agents of continuity and change. Moreover, it is interesting to observe that mothers or other female members of the family, in order to extract time for their domestic or agricultural roles or any other, transfer their adult workroles to their daughters, especially the eldest one in our studied cases. In fact, the young girls in the rural areas are deeply entrenched in their familial and non-familial activity, thereby, they become very involved and active in contributing significantly to the subsistence of their families. However, Neera Burra[1] observes that these girls are not taken so seriously because their work is not directly remunerative even if it is productive.

In our study we found that the young girls, irrespective of whether they are educated or uneducated, married or unmarried and coming from different caste and class background were performing several tasks, both within the household as well as outside. Tasks such as cooking, cleaning utensils, washing clothes, sibling care, homework study, cleaning the house, fetching water, looking after cattle, knitting and stitching, making beds, etc. are generally taken up by these young girls besides being casual workers in the fields and helping in sowing, weeding, harvesting, and threshing which happen to be seasonal activities. Without getting any formal training or skill, they perform these tasks sure-footedly.

The Household Work undertaken by Young Girls in Rural Areas

The accompanying tables (Table 8.1 and 8.2) present data in a general way to indicate the extent of involvement of the adolescent girls in various type of work activities. Here effort is also made to categorise the girls in terms of their being educated-uneducated, married/unmarried as related to the extent of involvement in 10 common types of work activities, by the pattern of their working time, number of hours of work, etc. A brief summary of the findings is also given below.

The tables present the data on the extent of involvement of adolescent girls in all the above given 10 types of work activities by their educated/uneducated, married/unmarried, pattern of working hours, by their caste status, and also village/statewise.

Out of the four hundred girls 62 per cent of the girls were cooking, 32 per cent girls were cleaning utensils and 24 per cent of them were washing clothes. Only 14.7 per cent were involved in sibling care. 29 per cent were taking care of the cattle and fodder and 10.7 per cent were doing their studies. Sixty per cent of them were cleaning the house regularly and 50.5 per cent were going to fetch water daily. Only 4.6 were busy knitting and stitching and 32 per cent plastered cowdung.

i) Cooking

Out of 248 girls who are cooking for their households, 124 girls are educated. Most of these girls come from the upper castes. About 140 girls spend 40 minutes to one hour on cooking. Whereas, 67 girls spend 40 to 60 minutes and 42 girls spend over an hour doing it. Eighty-one girls who are cooking are married and 142 girls are unmarried. Most of these girls either cook in the mornings or evenings. Only 13 girls cook in the afternoon.

Table 8.1: Work Pattern

Tasks	Category 1		Category 2						Category 3							
	Educated	Uneducated	U.C.	M.C.	L.C.	10-20 min.	20-40 min.	40-60 min.	60 & above	marrried	unmarried	morning	afternoon	evening	Total	%
Cooking	124	124	134	76	36	20	120	67	42	81	142	143	13	104	248	62
Cleaning utensils	60	69	19	39	68	16	42	46	16	36	90	86	25	42	129	32
Washing clothes	42	55	51	31	13	13	66	47	58	40	55	69	27	24	97	24
Sibling care	18	41	26	21	15	6	9	24	20	32	29	24	16	20	59	14
Looking after cattle	52	67	44	54	19	22	30	35	33	39	79	44	24	45	119	29
Studying,	43	-	28	11	4	-	12	24	8	4	35	10	21	11	43	10.7
cleaning the house	116	125	102	71	70	22	100	79	41	77	152	173	17	74	241	60.
Fetching water	85	117	78	59	26	42	46	66	45	41	161	161	26	104	202	50.5
Knitting and stitching	9	9	14	3	1	1	4	10	3	9	7	-	12	2	18	4.5
Plastering cowdung	55	74	62	36	31	14	36	32	45	58	71	89	13	20	129	32.0

Note: Differentials in different category totals is due to the fact that some of them did not respond to some specific questions.

We find that girls in Bharatpur and Jaunpur villages are cooking more often than those in the Delhi villages. Moreover, it is mostly in the morning that girls in Bharatpur villages do this task. Whereas, in Delhi and Jaunpur villages, they do both in the mornings and evenings. (see Table 8.2)

ii) Cleaning Utensils

Out of the 129 girls who are cleaning the utensils, 60 girls are educated and 69 girls are uneducated. Most of them come from the lower and middle castes. These girls spend from 20 minutes to more than an hour doing this task. Thirty-six girls who took up the above work are married, 90 unmarried and 86 are engaged in the morning also.

In Bharatpur villages, the lower caste girls generally spend about 40 minutes to an hour cleaning the utensils and most of them are married. Whereas, in Jaunpur villages, the girls who are performing this task are mostly married, uneducated and belong to the middle castes. However, in the Delhi villages it is all the married girls, mainly from the lower castes, who are cleaning utensils mostly in the evening (see Table 8.3).

iii) Washing Clothes

Out of 97 girls who engage in washing clothes, 42 girls are educated and 55 uneducated. Most of them belong to the upper and middle castes. They generally spend 20 minutes to over an hour daily doing this chore. Four girls out of the above-mentioned number are married and 55 are unmarried. Sixty-nine girls wash clothes in the morning; 27 in the afternoon and 24 in the evening.

Educated girls in Delhi villages wash clothes in the afternoon and evening. Whereas in Bharatpur villages, 22 uneducated girls wash clothes in the mornings and afternoons, and most of them are unmarried. In Bharatpur villages, however, both educated and uneducated girls, belonging mainly to the upper and middle castes, spend more than an hour washing clothes and half of them are married. Most of them wash clothes in the morning; 10 girls in the afternoon and 19 girls in the evening (see Table 8.2).

iv) Sibling Care

Out of the 59 girls who were involved in sibling care, 18 girls are educated and 41 girls are uneducated, who belong mainly to the upper and middle castes and only some to the lower castes. They generally spend one hour or more on taking care of their younger brothers or sisters. Thirty-two of the girls who are married did these tasks in their natal family and 29 girls who have this responsibility in their hands are unmarried. It is in the morning, afternoon and evening that they look after their siblings. This clearly shows how it helps the mothers to release themselves for other types of work both within and outside the house.

In the Delhi villages, however, we did not come across cases of sibling care. This may be explained by the fact that most of the girls here were school going girls. Nevertheless, in our group discussions, some of the girls did mention about it only on being asked. In Jaunpur villages, girls took care of their siblings in the afternoon, whereas, in Bharatpur villages, the girls took care of their brothers or sisters in the morning and evening and very few girls in the afternoon.

v) Tending of Cattle

Out of 199 girls who are looking after cattle and fodder, 52 girls are educated and 67 girls are uneducated; 39 married and 79 girls are unmarried. Almost half of these girls spend upto 40 minutes on this task, whereas, the other half spends an hour or more on it. Most of them do it in the morning (44) or evening (45), whereas, only 24 girls take care of the cattle in the afternoon. It also involves giving them a bath.

However, this work is being taken up mainly by the girls in Bharatpur and Jaunpur villages. In the Delhi villages, only one girl from the lower caste seems to be doing it. This may be explained by the impact of the urban environment. Most of the girls in Bharatpur villages who performed this task were unmarried (58) and in Jaunpur villages, both married (32) and unmarried girls (20) were involved in it.

vi) Studying

This includes doing home work and non-curricular reading. Only 43 girls were involved in studying and perceived it as a task. All of them are educated and belong mainly to the upper and middle castes. Only 4 girls out of them belong to the lower castes. These girls spend 20 minutes to over an hour studying daily. Most of these girls are unmarried and only 4 married girls invest their labour in studying.

Most of these girls are either from the Delhi villages or Jaunpur villages. Very few girls (9), who are studying belong to the villages of Bharatpur. It was in the morning that girls took up their studies in Bharatpur villages, wheras , in Delhi and Jaunpur areas it was mainly in the afternoon and evening (see Table 8.2).

vii) Cleaning the House

241 girls were doing the task of cleaning the house. Of these, 116 girls were educated and 125 girls uneducated. Most of them were from the upper and middle castes, (102 and 71 respectively); 70 however, were from the lower castes. All the girls spent at least 40 minutes in performing the above task; 120 girls spent an hour or more. Seventy-seven of these girls were married and 152 girls unmarried. This work was generally done in the morning. However, 74 girls did it in the evening and 17 girls in the afternoon.

In the Bharatpur and Jaunpur villages both the educated and the uneducated girls cleaned the house, whereas, in the Delhi villages this task was taken up mostly by the educated girls. It was mostly in the morning and at times in the evening in the Bharatpur villages, whereas, in Jaunpur villages, it was both in the morning and evening that these girls had this task in hand. (see Table 8.2)

viii) Fetching Water

Nearly 202 girls have the task of fetching water for the family. Of these 85 girls were educated and 117 uneducated. Most of them belong to the upper and middle castes except in the villages of Bharatpur, where many also belong to the lower castes. These girls spend from 20 minutes to over an hour each time in carrying water to their homes. Most of these girls were unmarried; only 41 are married. They generally went to fetch the water either in the morning or in the evening with a few exceptions, who went in the afternoon.

In the villages of Delhi, the girls who went to fetch water were generally educated, whereas, in the villages of Bharatpur and Jaunpur, both the educated and uneducated girls performed this task. Unmarried girls in Bharatpur villages and both, married and unmarried girls in Jaunpur villages took up this task (see Table 8.2).

ix) Knitting and Stitching

Only 18 girls were involved in knitting and stitching. They were both educated and uneducated and predominantly from the upper castes. They spent an hour or more doing it. Half of them were married. The girls generally took up this task in the afternoon, with the exception of 2 girls who did it in the evening. Most of the girls who were doing the above task belonged to the villages of Jaunpur (see Table 8.2). These girls were taking care of the family needs for wollens.

x) Plastering Cowdung

Over 129 girls were engaged in plastering cowdung (i.e. plastering the walls and surfacing the floors of their huts) or making the cow-dung cakes. Fifty-five of these girls were educated and 74 girls uneducated. Most of them belonged to the upper and middle castes and some to the lower castes (31). They spent 20 minutes to over an hour doing this task. Fifty-eight of these girls were married and 70 unmarried. They generally took up this task in the mornings. Very few girls did it either in the afternoon or evenings. These girls generally belonged to the villages of Bharatpur and Jaunpur; very few girls took it up in the villages of Delhi. This could be explained by the fact that most of the houses in the villages surrounding Delhi are 'pacca' (see Table 8.3).

It is interesting to see that majority of the girls said that male members do not help them in the household work. On being asked why, they said, "It is not their work" - they are not expected to do it as it is a 'woman's task'.

Thus 70.75 per cent girls did not get any assistance from male members in the household tasks. Only 8.75 per cent have some sort of help, whereas, 20.50 per cent don't ask for any help from others. It is this passive acceptance of gender based division of work which must be emphasized and questioned here.

Even if all this amounts to making these girls contribute significantly to the amelioration of their family situation, yet, it is seen as burdensome by a number of girls. This can also be viewed as a situation of overwork in the sense that these young girls are not mature enough, (physically and mentally), to take up many of these tasks simultaneously, especially when they are also attending school. Psychologically, there is an unpreparedness on the part of these girls to take up adult roles which are transferred to them consciously or unconsciously by their mothers. This somehow does not leave the girls with any social space and personal time that could allow the phenomena of adolescence to occur. Moreover, the mothers and

Table 8.2: Work Pattern

Area	Edu-cated	Non-edu.	U.C.	M.C.	L.C.	10-20 min.	20-40 min.	40-60 min.	60 and above	mar-ried	unmar-ried	morn-ing	after-noon	even-ing	
Delhi	14	7	3	12	6	1	8	12	-	7	15	8	1	12	
Bharatpur	42	85	46	52	29	12	58	30	27	28	99	103	5	72	cooking
Jaunpur	68	32	85	12	1	7	54	25	15	46	28	32	7	20	
Delhi	12	5	3	3	11	2	13	2	-	7	10	1	3	13	cleaning
Bharatpur	35	48	12	18	52	8	30	29	13	9	72	63	16	18	utensils
Jaunpur	13	16	4	18	5	6	9	15	3	20	8	22	6	11	
Delhi	7	2	4	5	-	-	4	2	3	5	6	2	4	3	
Bharatpur	13	22	11	13	9	12	58	30	27	8	23	27	13	2	washing
Jaunpur	22	31	36	13	4	1	4	15	28	27	26	40	10	19	clothes
Delhi	-	-	-	-	-	-	-	-	-	-	-	-	-	-	sibling
Bharatpur	11	29	18	12	12	6	7	20	8	22	18	21	9	16	care
Jaunpur	7	12	8	9	3	-	2	4	12	10	11	3	7	4	
Delhi	1	-	-	-	1	-	-	1	1	1	1	-	-	-	looking
Bharatpur	19	48	21	32	13	19	17	19	12	57	58	34	23	23	after
Jaunpur	32	19	23	22	5	3	13	15	21	32	220	10	3	22	cattle

Table 8.2 continued

Delhi	19	-	12	5	2	-	10	6	3	1	14	-	13	6	studying
Bharatpur	9	-	6	3	-	-	-	7	2	2	7	7	1	1	
Jaunpur	15	-	10	3	2	-	2	11	3	1	14	3	7	4	
Delhi	15	5	4	13	3	-	8	3	9	7	12	11	2	3	cleaning the house
Bharatpur	53	85	34	43	62	20	59	34	26	20	107	115	10	43	
Jaunpur	48	35	64	15	5	2	33	42	6	50	33	47	5	28	
Delhi	7	0	-	5	2	-	3	4	-	2	5	4	-	3	fetching the water
Bharatpur	65	96	51	48	23	38	40	50	30	20	141	134	14	88	
Jaunpur	13	21	27	6	1	4	3	12	15	19	15	23	12	13	
Delhi	2	-	2	-	-	-	-	2	-	2	-	-	-	-	knitting and stitching
Bharatpur	2	2	2	1	1	-	1	2	1	2	-	-	3	-	
Jaunpur	5	7	10	2	-	1	3	6	2	5	7	-	7	2	
Delhi	4	3	1	5	2	-	3	2	2	2	5	-	-	-	surfacing cowdung or plastering cowdung
Bharatpur	13	29	5	13	24	9	13	12	6	15	27	36	-	3	
Jaunpur	38	42	56	18	5	5	20	18	37	41	39	53	13	17	

Table 8.3: Participation in Work Activities by Educational Status

	Total	cooking	cleaning utensils	washing clothes	sibling care	looking after cattle	studying	cleaning the house	fetching water	knitting and stitching	surfacing/ cowdung cake making
Educated girls in the sample	265	(124)	(60)	(42)	(18)	(52)	(43)	(116)	(85)	(9)	(55)
Delhi		14	12	7	-	-	19	15	7	2	4
Bharatpur		42	35	13	11	19	9	53	65	2	13
Jaunpur		68	13	22	7	32	15	48	13	5	38
Uneducated girls in the sample	135	(187)	(29)	(55)	(43)	(67)	-	(125)	(117)	(9)	(74)
Delhi		7	5	2	-	-	-	5	0	-	3
Bharatpur		85	48	22	29	48	-	85	96	2	29
Jaunpur		32	16	31	12	19	-	35	21	7	42

Table 8.4: Participation in Work Activities by Marital Status

	Total	cooking	cleaning utensils	washing clothes	sibling care	looking after cattle	studying	cleaning the house	fetching water	knitting and stitching	surfacing/ cowdung cake making
Married girls in the sample	(87)	(81)	(36)	(40)	(32)	(39)	(4)	(77)	(41)	(9)	(58)
Delhi	10	7	7	5	-	-	1	7	2	2	2
Bharatpur	18	28	9	8	22	7	2	20	20	2	15
Jaunpur	59	46	20	27	10	32	1	50	19	5	41
Unmarried girls in the sample	(313)	(142)	(90)	(55)	(29)	(79)	(35)	(152)	(161)	(7)	(71)
Delhi	60	15	10	6	-	1	14	12	5	-	5
Bharatpur	180	99	72	23	18	58	7	107	141	-	27
Jaunpur	73	28	8	26	11	20	14	33	15	7	39

Table 8.5: Participation in Work Activities by Caste Status

	Total	cooking	cleaning utensils	washing clothes	sibling care	looking after cattle	studying	cleaning the house	fetching water	knitting and stitching	surfacing/ cowdung cake making
Upper Caste girls	(198)	(134)	(19)	(51)	(26)	(44)	(28)	(102)	(78)	(14)	(62)
Delhi		3	3	4	-	-	12	4	-	2	1
Bharatpur		46	12	11	18	21	6	34	51	2	5
Jaunpur		85	4	36	8	23	10	64	27	10	56
Middle Caste girls	(104)	(79)	(29)	(31)	(21)	(54)	(11)	(71)	(59)	(3)	(36)
Delhi		15	3	5	-	-	5	13	5	-	5
Bharatpur		52	18	13	12	32	3	43	48	1	13
Jaunpur		12	8	13	9	22	3	15	6	2	18
Lower Caste girls	(87)	(36)	(68)	(13)	(15)	(19)	(5)	(70)	(26)	(1)	(31)
Delhi		6	11	-	-	1	2	3	2	-	2
Bharatpur		29	52	9	12	13	1	62	23	1	24
Jaunpur		1	5	4	3	5	2	5	1	-	5

Note: Out of the 400 girls, 7 were Muslims and 4 did not respond to the question on caste. Thus this sample refers to only 389 girls. Caste descriptions were based on conventional classifications relevant in the villages.

female members of the family do not perceive these girls as productive workers since there seems to be no direct financial gain and then, socio-culturally, it is something which is part of the inbuilt expectation - system in rural areas. Although these young girls perform varied tasks, they do not derive any self confidence from such work. The mothers are taken as role-models and these young girls inherit their work roles from their mothers and other female numbers of the family.

Table 8.6: Help from Male members in Household tasks

No help	70.75 per cent
Some help	8.75 per cent
Don't ask for help	20.50 per cent
Total	**100.00**

Table 8.7: Parent's Response on the Type of Work

	Pattern	Per cent of parents' response
1.	No response	1.5
2.	Don't know	-
3.	Yes, Girls should work as boys do	75.00
4.	No, girls should not work like boys	20.50
5.	Girls should work like boys only if there is a need	3.00
	Total	**100.00**

On being asked whether the girls should do the same type of work as that of boys, 75 per cent of parents responded in the affirmative and 20.5 per cent in the negative. Only 3 per cent of the parents felt that girls should work like boys in case there is a necessity or emergency. Even though the parents expressed the wish that their sons and daughters perform similar tasks, yet, in reality the girls end up doing most of the household chores.

We also observed that generally the burden of the household work such as cooking, cleaning, washing clothes, fetching water, etc., falls mainly on the eldest sister, whereas, the younger brothers and sisters are sent to school. For instance, in Kishangarh, Manju, besides working at home, is employed as a maid also. This leaves her with no time for attending school. Zareena in Rangpuri too was forced to drop out of school by her parents since a great amount of work had to be taken care of at home. Similarly in Sewar, many girls were not sent to the school by their parents as there was no one else to cook, clean, fetch the water and look after the cattle. In Malipura, whereas, they even worked on the farms during the sowing, cultivating and harvesting period. In Jaunpur almost all the girls, excepting the upper caste and economically well to do family girls, worked as farm labourers to supplement the family income.

To the question on whether the girls should work after being educated, 86 per cent of the parents responded in the affirmative. Only 5 per cent of parents did not want their daughters to work and 7.5 per cent of the parents had left this decision to allow the girls to work on their in-laws. This clearly indicates the attitudinal change of the parents regarding their daughters' education. Most of them link her education with some sort of remuneration.

Table 8.8: Parents' response on the girl's work-role in future

	Pattern	Per cent of parents' response
1.	No response	1.5
2.	Don't know	-
3.	Will not work after being educated	5.0
4.	Will work after being educated	86.0
5.	Depends upon her in-laws	7.5
	Total	**100.00**

In Nogayan, girls mentioned being beaten up by their mothers in case they refused to work at home. Many girls in the villages of Delhi also experienced the same. The school going girls all over generally worked at home either before leaving for school or after coming back from the school either in the afternoon or evening.

Table 8.9: Leisure Available to the Girls in Rural Area

	Pattern	Per cent of girl
1.	No response	3.5
2.	No leisure	24.5
3.	Leisure in the morning	9.25
4.	Leisure in the afternoon	33.25
5.	Leisure in the evening	24.00
6.	Leisure in the late-evening	5.5
	Total	**100.00**

24.5 per cent of girls in our sample did not get any leisure time, whereas, 9.25 per cent got some free time in the mornings. 33.25 per cent had some leisure in the afternoons and 24 per cent in the evenings. Many of these girls spent their leisure either sleeping, resting, chatting with their friends, watching T.V. or listening to the radio.

The tables on work pattern indicate that it is evidently in the afternoons that these girls have some time at hand which can be utilized for creative purposes.

Hence, we can safely infer from the evidence presented in this section that it is the eldest daughter who generally pays the price for the opportunities that the younger brothers or sisters avail of in the rural areas. The double load of the domestic and the non-domestic work leaves no time for her to attend school, nor an opportunity to read, and often she drops out of school if she is at all enrolled. It is not necessarily the eldest daughter in the family alone but younger girls too are denied any schooling at all, just because there are household chores to be done. Not only this, but this burden of work hampers the physical, intellectual and psychological growth of these girls because, as it is, they rarely get an adequate nutritional support at home, for various reasons. Even during their sickness they are not being given proper medical attention. All these factors combined together have an adverse effect on their levels of learning and prepares them poorly for their adult life. It is ironic to find that the performance of workroles prematurely remains unperceived by elders, who force the young girls to comply with the age old traditions.

Chapter Nine

Her Dreams and Desires: The Promised Land

"What do you aspire to be in life? What do you wish to possess? What do you want to learn?" Just these three questions elicited numerous answers. They varied from such profound ones as 'I want to possess knowledge' to the very simple, down-to-earth wish to visit the Taj Mahal or have a *Sundar Dulha* or 'a mother-in-law who would do all the work rather than command and demand work'!

In our sample we had some respondents who didn't know what they wanted to be. There were others who could articulate quite precisely what they aspire to be but didn't have the required information to reach their goals.

Table 9.1: Future Expectation of Girls - Employment types

	10-12	12-14	14-16	Total	Percentage
No response	10	13	37	60	15.00
Do not know	5	15	35	55	13.75
Teacher	21	37	103	161	40.25
Typist	2	5	13	20	5.00
Nurse	3	2	11	16	4.00
Housewife	4	5	36	45	11.25
Police Officer	0	3	3	6	1.05
Collector	0	0	2	2	0.50
Tailor	0	3	9	12	3.00
Doctor	1	1	21	23	5.75

Whereas 15 per cent of the girls did not respond, 13.75 per cent did not know what they wanted to be. However, a majority of 40.25 per cent said they want to be school teachers, followed by 11.25 per cent who want to be housewives. About 5.75 per cent wanted to be doctors and 5 per cent wanted to be tailors. Only 1.5 per cent and 0.5 per cent wanted to be a Police Officer and a Collector, respectively.

Let us look at the majority who want to be teachers. What are the options open to a girl in the village situation? The only profession she knows about is being a teacher. But why just this? Looking at the village situation, we find that teaching is treated as a noble profession - something which a woman 'can or is allowed' to do. It is one, of the many traditional options 'reserved' for women. Therefore, in being a teacher she will not be flouting any established norm - she in fact, fits in well into 'what a woman can do'. This, also highlights the fact that these girls don't have the required information nor do they get opportunities to do other kinds of jobs. They do not know they 'can' do other jobs as well. Moreover, even those who expressed the choice of being one or the other of these do not know how they can be done. They have no information about courses/degrees which would entitle them to be either a teacher or a nurse or a doctor or many other vocation.

In this context it is significant to assess the degree to which the family members working outside the village influence the girl's choice of profession by either being a direct or indirect source of information. In our sample many girls were motivated by their fathers, brothers or uncles. Thus, Kavita at Kishangarh wants to be a nurse "because her uncle works as an electrician in Girdharilal hospital". Similarly, Sunita and Rekha at Rangpuri want to be doctors or engineers. Their father is a computer engineer.

Out of the 40.25 per cent who said they wanted to be teachers, most of the girls were from the age-group 14-16 years (103/161 = 63.97 per cent) and from upper caste (9/161 = 55.90 per cent). Only (13/161 = 20.5 per cent) are from the middle and (36/161 = 22.36 per cent) from the lower castes. There are two Muslim girls (1.24 per cent). This may indicate another norm of 'teaching' as a profession being restricted to upper castes and particularly the Brahmins. Moreover, most of these girls are educated, 95 (59 per cent) being from middle and above levels. Twenty-five are from primary level and 17 are uneducated. This may, on the other hand, indicate and quite convincingly the positive role education is playing in helping girls formulate and articulate what they want to be. From the table given below we can see that out of those who wish to just remain housewives and not take up a job, 15 are uneducated and 18 are educated only upto primary.

Table 9.2: Future Expectation of Employment types by Educational Levels

	Uned-ucated	Upto Prim.	Upto midd.	Upto sec.	Upto Hy.sec.	Total
No Response	27	22	3	4	4	60
Don't know	14	18	9	9	5	55
Teacher	17	35	53	45	11	161
Typist	3	2	7	4	4	20
Nurse	1	5	6	2	2	16
Housewife	15	18	7	2	3	45
Police Officer	0	1	2	2	1	6
Collector	0	1	0	1	0	2
Tailor	3	2	4	2	1	12
Doctor	1	13	1	13	7	23
Total						**400**

Out of the girls who were not able to tell us about their ambitions, the majority were either uneducated (14) or had studied only upto primary level (18). Even those who did not respond come from a similar educational background.

Though the ambition of becoming a teacher is common to all the three areas, in Delhi, none of the girls wanted to be a housewife, whereas, in Bharatpur and Jaunpur villages, after teaching the maximum response was to be a housewife. In fact at Kishangarh in Delhi, Bhateri expressed quite strongly that she would either be a telephone operator or a nurse and wouldn't marry for she may be beaten up by her in-laws. This may indicate the influence of the urban culture on the villages near Delhi. Although it may not be absolute, the desire to work, to be employed and be independent is quite strong among these girls. After being educated they wish to move out of the household premises and engage in economically gainful activities.

On being asked what did they want most to possess or do if given a chance, most of them (36.75 per cent) expressed the desire to possess some material article like trinkets or a pair of new dress or shoes, etc. The majority of these respondents were from Rajasthan. Whereas 89 girls said they want to have a peaceful life, 36 wanted to 'get education'. Only 16 wished to travel. Thirteen did not know what they want and 41 didn't want anything.

All those who wanted a 'peaceful life', were from Bharatpur (46) and Jaunpur (43) villages. By 'peaceful' these girls meant an easy life with less work. None of the girls from Delhi said 'peaceful life' in this sense. This may be due to the fact that school going girls in Delhi are not asked to do a major share of the household work unlike the rural girls of Bharatpur and Jaunpur villages.

Further, it is interesting to note that of the girls who want to pursue education, most of them are already going to the school (21 out of 36). Both educated and uneducated girls expressed the desire to travel. Similarly, the wish to possess some material article is common to both educated and uneducated girls. They expressed the wish to possess a gold chain, a pair of anklets, bangles, a new set of clothes, chappals, shoes, etc.

Table 9.3: Future Expectations -- General by Educational Status

	Uned-ucated	Upto Prim.	Upto midd.	Upto sec	Upto Hy.sec.	Total	%
No response	24	15	10	4	5	58	14.50
Don't know	6	6	1	0	0	13	3.25
Nothing	12	6	6	14	3	41	10.25
Education	1	4	16	10	5	36	9.00
Material things	32	46	33	24	12	147	36.75
Travel	1	5	5	3	2	16	4.00
Peaceful life	1	19	20	40	9	89	22.25

Most of those who said they did not know what they wanted were uneducated. However, there are some (41) who, irrespective of either being educated or uneducated were quite contented with whatever they had.

In our sample the girls had a variety of ambitions and wishes to 'possess' different things in life. But there is one thing almost all - wished to do, i.e. learn knitting and stitching. On being asked what would they like to learn, irrespective of their age, caste, educational status - they not merely reflect but even confirm that a woman should learn just these tasks which have been traditionally assigned to them. Out of 400 girls, 331 i.e. 82.75 per cent want to learn knitting and stitching.

Table 9.4: Future Aspirations and Deisre of the girls

	AGE GROUP				
	10-12	12-14	14-16	Total	Percentage
No Response	4	6	11	21	5.25
Don't Know	4	4	1	9	2.25
Stitching	6	10	45	61	15.25
Knitting	25	53	192	270	67.50
Reading	1	0	2	3	0.75
Handicraft	3	2	7	12	3.00
Learn about health and hygiene matters and her body	4	5	9	18	4.00
Music	1	2	3	6	1.50
Total				**400**	**100.00**

In their wishes, aspiration and desire to learn, these girls reflect the stereotyped image of what a woman can and should learn. This is due to their lack of information, less exposure and awareness and the absence of a scientific attitude towards other roles they can perform in life.

Moreover, if we go by the majority's desire to learn just knitting and stitching, we would be perpetuating the process of this stereotyping of 'women's skills and roles'. These girls, who are our focus of attention, need to learn, know and perform much more than just knitting and stitching. In order to be a better person, to improve her self-image, to get time and opportunity to learn about herself, her family, her society, an integrated and comprehensive programme is proposed in the Appendix.

Notes

Chapter One

1 See *Encyclopedia Britanica*, 1951, Vol. I, pp. 171-72
2 Erick H. Erickson, *Identity, Youth and Crisis* (New York: W.W. Norton, 1968).
3 A.B. Hollingshead, "Some Crucial Tasks Facing Youth: Problems of Adolescence, Peer Group and Early Marriage", in R.K. MacIver,ed., *Dilemmas of Youth in America Today* (New York: Harper & Brothers, 1961), pp. 15-30.
4 Hans Sebald, *Adolescence - A Social Psychological Analysis* (New Jersey: Prentice Hall, 1968), p. 7.
5 Ibid., p. 22.
6 Pauline K. Garg and Indira J. Parikh, *Profiles of Identity* (Ahmedabad: Academic Book Centre, 1976), Chapter Two.
7 J.J. Meyer, *Sexual Life in Ancient India* (New York: Barnes and Noble, 1953), Chapter "The Maid".
8 Shanti Ghosh, "Discrimination Begins at Birth", Paper presented to the Workshop "Focus on the Girl Child", 1985, p. 3.
9 UNICEF, "An Analysis of the Situation of Children India", 1984, p. 31, Table 20.
10 *Survey of Causes of Death* (Rural), Annual Report 1983; Series 3, No. 16 (New Delhi: Office of the Registrar General, 1985), pp. 6-7.
11 *Survey of Causes of Death* (Rural), Office of the Registrar General, 1980.
12 Muriel Wasi, "Women and Education", Paper presented to the Workshop on the Girl Child, National Media Centre and UNICEF, Delhi 1985.
13 O.P. Sharma and Robert D. Retherford, *Recent Literacy Trends in India*, New Delhi: Office of the Registrar General of India), p. 11.
14 Rami Chhabra, et. al., "Health and Demographic Consequences of Early Marriage and Fertility," *Social Change*, September 1987.
15 Indian Council of Medical Research, *Growth and Physical Development of Indian Infants and Children*, Technical Report Series, no. 18, 1984.

Chapter Four

1 The sample is tilted towards the 14-16 age group and to some extent towards the 12-14 age group. This fact has been explained in the section on methodology. Further, majority of our respondents were the first child of their families (the eldest) as shown in Table 4.10. Girls who did not respond when asked may be because they did not know their age. Leela Dube, "On the Construction of Gender: Hindu Girls in a Patrilineal India", Paper presented to NIPCCD Workshop on the Girl Child, December 1987.
2 Ibid.
3 Ibid., p. 19.

Chapter Five

1 Leela Dube, "On the Construction of Gender: Hindu Girls in Patrilineal India",

Paper presented at National Workshop on Girl Child, NIPCCD, New Delhi, December 1987.

2 Ibid.

Chapter Six

1 H. Sebald, *Adolescence - A Social Psychological Analysis* (New Jersey: Prentice Hall, 1968).

2 Parsons and Bales, "Family Structure and the Socialisation of the Child", in *Family, Socialization and Interaction Process* (Glencoe: Free Press, 1955).

3 Leela Dube, "On Construction of Gender: Hindu Girls in Patrilineal India," Paper presented at National Workshop on the Girl Child, NIPCCD, New Delhi, December 1987, p. 11.

Appendix

Programme Design for Overall Development of Rural Adolescent Girls

Our study has amply brought out the harsh reality that the 'adolescent girls' are a distinct lot entirely different from the other age groups of female population. They are essentially those falling in the age group between 10 and 16 years. They are the future mothers and in all probability will form part of economically active population. They are thus likely to be the core of human resource available in the country.

In any development vision such core group of population cannot be ignored or kept isolated. Our study has also brought out with strong evidence that problems, needs and aspiration of the adolescent girls are distinct and separate. Their problems and needs cannot be clubbed with children or women. There is, therefore, a strong need to have a developmental programme meant and directed specifically for the overall enhancement of the adolescent girls in the villages of India.

It is a fact that a number of developmental programmes are under implementation across the country to benefit the women at large. They include IRDP, TRYSEM, DWCRA, STEP, STAD and ICDS. A brief picture about the target groups, objectives and beneficiaries of these programmes is highlighted in a comparative manner in Table 11.1. It is evident that none of these programmes cover the needs of the adolescent girls in rural areas. Unfortunately, girls in the age group 10 and 16 years are completely missing from the focus of these programmes.

Table 1: A Comparative Display of Developmental Programme

	TRYSEM	IRDP DWCRA	STEP	CSWB Condensed Course	CSWB Vocational Training	ICDS
1. Target group	Rural youth from families below poverty line	Women and children in rural areas from families below poverty line	Employed rural women and those seeking employment	Adult women particularly in rural areas	Adult women	Children
2. Age Group	18-35 years		Adult women	18-30	18-30/ minimum age being flexible to include 16 years	0-6
3. Beneficiaries	Rural families below poverty line 30 per cent should be SC/ST and 30 per cent should be women	Women as a group and not as individuals	Adult women	Both illiterate and neo-literate women	Needy and deserving women	*Direct:* mother, pregnant women, children *Indirect:* adolescent girl

Table 1 continued

	TRYSEM	IRDP DWCRA	STEP	CSWB Condensed Course	CSWB Vocational Training	ICDS
4. Objectives	1. Provide technical skills; 2. Self employment in: (a)agriculture allied activities; (b)industries; (c)services; (d)business activities	1. To provide income generating activities in order to enhance the economic and nutritional status of family; 2. To provide an organisational support in terms of a delivery system of goods and services available in one of the covered areas	To launch action projects to improve women's employment in (a) agriculture (b) dairy, (c) animal husbandry (d) handloom	1. Open up new vistas of employment to a large number to needy and deserving women; 2. Create a band of competent trained workers to man various social development projects	1. To train selected vocations for employment/ self employment	Child protection and development: (a) reduce LBW and severe malnutrition; (b) reduce school drop-outs rates (c) reduce mortality morbidity rates; (d) provide the environmental conditions for the mental, physical & social development of children; (e) enhance mothers' capability for proper child-care

Problem Areas of Adolescent Girls

Looking into the problems and needs of the rural adolescent girls, we have clearly indicated certain areas of concern which need immediate attention of the policy makers, planners and agencies/organisations working out at the village level for improving the lot of most neglected and deprived sections of the Indian society. They are most deprived because they suffer from not only poverty but also gender bias. They are discriminated against both within the family and outside for the sheer fact of their sex. Some of the problem areas of adolescent girls identified in the study are as under:

1. Girls generally did not approve of marriage at an early age, but they would not speak against the wishes of their parents, let alone defy them without tragic consequences;
2. Their mobility was severely restricted, especially after attaining puberty. As a result, most of them had to discontinue their education;
3. They were overburdened with workload at a tender age when the body needs maximum care for growth and personality development. In many a case, they had hardly any time to play;
4. Surprisingly, most of girls were not aware of child bearing and rearing practices. This can lead to difficult motherhood and also adds to high rate of infant mortality and morbidity;
5. Girls were also found to be completely unaware of the uses of banks, post offices and transport systems;
6. The formal education, even in a limited scale, had not changed the attitude of these girls on traditions and social customs;
7. Girls, by and large, had a very low, self image. This was due to the fact that they were always made to believe that their bodies are impure after puberty and that girls are weak and inferior, and always an object of attraction for males. They lack self confidence too;
8. Most of the girls preferred a small family. But they were not aware of the birth control measures;
9. They were not well informed about their body and bodily

functions;

10. Parents were found to be as ignorant as their daughters in many cases. On many issues, they rigidly adhered to orthodoxy of traditions and social norms;
11. Social evils like dowry was not liked by girls and some parents too. But, parents were giving dowry in marriage of their daughters just because others in the society practiced it, largely to maintain their social status and acceptibility. Interestingly, many of the girls saw rationale of dowry in the absence of share in parental property;
12. Drop outs among girls were relatively high, especially by the time girls attained puberty. This was largely due to the insecurity regarding sexual harassment of the girls in the minds of parents;
13. Though some of these girls were also working on family farm or helping mothers as agricultural workers in harvesting and weeding, they were not aware of modern agricultural operations and practices.
14. They hardly have any leisure. Even if they find time, there are hardly any facilities available for girls in the villages for entertainment.
15. There was discrimination in food and nutrition given to these growing young girls. Moreover, girls as well as the parents, were not aware of the nutritional requirements.

Suggested Programme

In view of multi-faceted problems of the growing young girls and non-coverage of these girls under any of the existing programmes, we strongly recommend the implementation of an exclusive programme for the benefit of the adolescent girls in rural areas. Since, the problems and needs/aspirations of these girls revolve more around gender bias, social discriminations and lack of general awareness, the intended programme has to be oriented, towards benefiting these girls in a holistic manner. Such a programme has to have an integrated multi-dimensional approach with building up of awareness, education for equality, training in health care, skill training for self-employment/employment, providing secretarial facilities to them, and improving the accessibility of available technologies.

This programme can be given the name *Parivartan Kishori Vikas Pariyojana* (PKVP).

Objectives of the Programme

The objective of the programme is to facilitate a holistic development of the rural young girls. This involves development at various levels of her body, her person, her work, her family and her village community in networking with the rest of the system. She should be treated not just as a future mother or a future worker, but a person. Such a programme is required not only because the rural young girls belong to a hitherto deprived and neglected section but also because they are almost totally missing from any existing governmental or non-governmental programmes. The specific objective of the programme will be as following:

1. Improve health status of the young girls,
2. Increase educational level of young girls,
3. Delay early marriage, providing knowledge of childbirth contraception and childcare.
4. Improve work conditions of the girls by introducing appropriate technology for household work,
5. Providing them with recreational facilities for (a) games, (b) music, dance and play, (c) village libraries, (d) Yoga and other exercises, (e) drawing, painting, clay modelling and (f) gardening;
6. Development of skills for self-employment.
7. Improve their understanding of their bodily functions and help them enhance the self-image and self-confidence,
8. Increase awareness regarding society and politics,
9. Reorient and motivate parents to overcome socio-cultural constraints,
10. Improve their mobility by organising camps, melas and study tours through schools.

Keeping the above objectives we propose a comprehensive programme essentially to give these girls space to grow. Because their development is not independent of or in isolation from their place in the family and village community, programmes must aim at overcoming existing structural (situation of poverty and scarcity) and social (negative attitudes) constraints as well.

Target Group
The programme would cover growing young girls in the age group of 10-16 years in the rural areas.

Programme Components
The programme visualises realisation of set objective through establishment of 'Kishori Kendra' in each village with a few trained women staff who could implement the programme.

Infrastructural Facilities
The Kishori Kendras must be equipped with: (a) *Parivartan Pustakalaya*, (b) TV and videos, (c) playground with swings and other open air games facilities, and (d) skill raising equipments, (e) other educational equipments like blackboards, counting boards, etc.

The *Kendras* should conduct short courses for

a) awareness, education for equality to make these girls understand social, cultural and structural constraints and gender inequalities and help the girls utilise the acquired knowledge,
b) health and hygiene education to help them understand their bodies and bodily functions, menstrual cycle, marital behaviour, personal hygiene, water uses to prevent water-borne diseases, direct or oral rehydration therapy, importance of vaccinations and preventive medicines, and
c) extending information and knowledge about surroundings, structural facilities like bank, post office, hospitals, bus station, railway station, etc. These courses should also be followed by refresher courses and care should be taken to organise these courses during lean seasons when girls are relatively free.

Creative Activities

1. Girls should be encouraged to undertake creative activities like clay modelling, knitting, stitching, drawing and painting;

2. Group functions like melas for collective expressions of joy and excitement should be organised on regular intervals at village level,

3. Study tours, excursions and learning through travel should be organised for such girls;

4. Games and physical exercises like Yoga should be encouraged;

5. Folk music, dance and theatre should be organised on regular intervals and girls must be encouraged to actively participate in all such events.

Skill Training

Skill training should strictly be linked with need activities that are based and which match the aptitude and abilities of the girl. Information about the use of improved technologies in agriculture should also be imparted to such girls.

Implementing Machinery

The programme may involve substantial financial commitments and trained women power requirements. It may be implemented in a phased manner by selecting a few districts and village therefrom in the initial stage on pilot basis. To start with NGOs, should be encouraged to implement model projects. In the first phase, implementation of the programme may be sought through the existing structure of ICDS schemes.

Supportive Efforts

The Government must launch a media campaign to help improve the status of growing young girls in rural areas by conveying messages through television, radio and local newspapers on issues like nutritional needs of the girls, evil effect of early marriage on the health of the girl, against child abuse, and project an image of a self-confident and strong girl instead of a shy and weak girl.

Legislation for Protection of Children's Right

A legislation should be brought to protect children against battering and child abuse. This is urgent because we have observed many instances of merciless child beating and extreme carelessness about child care.

Bibliography

Baig, Tara Ali, *Some Implications of Child Rearing Habits and Practices in India*, Delhi: National Media Centre and UNICEF, 1985.

Bezberuah, D.N., *The Girl Child in a Changing Society* National Media centre & UNICEF, 1985.

Bhattacharjee, Run, *The Girl Child, A Being that does not Exist for the Media* Delhi: National Media Centre * UNICEF 1985.

Beauchamp, Dubois, *Hindu Manners, Customs and Ceremonies* London: Oxford, 1953.

Buhler, G, (translated by) *The Sacred Books of the East, The Laws of Manu* Oxford, 1886.

Chambers Robert, *Rural Development* London: Longman 1983.

Chatterjee, Meera, *Both Gender and Age against them* Delhi: National Media Centre, UNICEF, 1985.

Desai, B.G., *The Emerging Youth* Bombay: Popular Prakashan, 1976

Encyclopedia Brittannica. 1951, Vol. 1.

Erik H. Erikson *Identity, Youth and Crisis*, New York: W.W. Norton, 1968.

Garg, Paulin K. and Indira J. Parikh, *Profiles in Identity* Ahmedabad: Academic Book Centre, 1976.

Ghosh, Shanti, *Discrimination Begins at Birth*, New Delhi: National Media Centre, UNICEF, 1985.

Gokhale, Sharad D. and Neera K. Sohoni, (ed.,) *Child in India* Bombay: Somaiya Publications, 1979.

Malik, Harji, "Interview with S Harcharan Singh," Delhi: National Media Centre, UNICEF, 1985.

Mishra, Ameeta, Amniocentesis, Law and the Female Chile" Delhi: National Media Centre, UNICEF, 1985.

Mankehar Purnima, "The Girl Child in India", Data Sheet on Health, Delhi: UNICEF, 1985.

Mukherjee, Nilanjana, 'Folklore and Proverbs from Bengal Related to the Girl Child'; Delhi: National Media Centre, UNICEF, 1985.

Jain, Kiran, "Personality Studies of Adolescent Girls" Ph.D Thesis, Allahabad University, 1955.

Jephertt, Agnes Pearl, *Girls Growing Up* London: Faber and Faber, 1942.

Joseph, G., Desrochers, J., Kalathil, M., *Health Care in India* Bangalore: Centre for Social Action, 1983.

Khanna, Girija, *Women: Sixteen to Sixty*, New Delhi: Vikas Publshers, New Delhi, 1975.

Kumari, R.B., "Personality Traits of Indian Adolescent Girls" D. Phil. Thesis, Allahabad University, 1954.

Kureshi, Afzal, *Adolescent Fantasy* Calcutta: Minerwa Associates, Calcutta, 1975.

Lewin Kurt, *A Dynamic, Theory of Personality* New York: McGraw Hill, 1935.

MacIver, R.K., (ed.,) *Dilemmas of Youth in America Today* Harper & Brothers, 1961.

Mead, Mrgaret, *Coming of Age in Samoa* New York: Morrow, 1928.

Mehta, Prayag, *The Indian Youth* Bombay: Somaiya Publications, 1971.

Meyer, J.J., *Sexual Life in Ancient Indian* New York, Barness & Nobel, 1953.

Moriarty, Alice E. and Povl W. Toussing, *Adolescent Coping*, New York, Grune & Straton, 1976.

Mukherjee, Dhurjati, ed.) *Youth: Change and Challenge* Calcutta: Firma KLM, 1977.

Namale, Meghmala, "Self Concept Among Adolescent Girls" Ph.D. Thesis, Poona University.

Nanda, Anant K., "The Psychological Needs of Adolescent Girls and their Bearing on Individual Adjustment", Ph.D. Thesis, Delhi Univeristy, 1957.

Nicholson, J. *What Society does to Girls* London: Virago, 1977.

Parsons and Bales, "Family Structure and the Socialization of the Child," in *Family, Socialization and Interaction Process*, Glencoe: Free Press, 1955.

Parthasarathi, Vibha, "Socialisation, women and Education: An Experiment", Delhi: National Media Centre and UNICEF, 1985.

Patel, Apurna, "Teenagers", *Indian Express*, 4 April, 1977, pp. 6-8.

Policies, Programmes, Schemes, Legislation and Statistics on Women, 1987, New Delhi: NIPPCD.

Pont, Ika Paul, *Child Welfare in India - An Integrated Approach*, Ministry of Education, Govt. of India, 1963.

Rai, Usha, "The Girl Child and the Media", Delhi: National Media Centre and UNICEF, 1985.

Recommendations on "Focus on the Girl Child", Delhi: UNICEF and National Media Centre, 1985.

Sandal, Veenu, "Schooling Brings a Change," Delhi: National Media Centre and UNICEF, 1985.

Saraswati, Malti, "A Comparative Study of the Personality Pattern of Adolescent Boys and Girls (14+ to 17+)," Ph.D. Thesis, Allahabad University, 1964.

Sebald, Hans, *Adolscence - A Social Psychological Analysis*, New Jersey: Prentice Hall, 1968.

Singh, R.G., *Rural Modernization: Contradiction and Change*, Delhi: Intellectual Publishing House, 1982.

Singh, Surya Nath and Pandey, N.N., "Status of Girl Child - Socio-economic Factors," Delhi: National Media Centre and UNICEF, 1985.

Wasi, Muriel, "Women and Education," Delhi: National Media Centre and UNICEF, 1985.

Wiesinger, Rita Ferris, "The Indian Adolscent Girls", Ph.D. Thesis, Bombay University, 1984.

Index